Career Progression Guide for Soldiers

A Practical Guide for Getting Ahead in Today's Competitive Army

4th Edition

Audie G. Lewis

STACKPOLE BOOKS

0 11557 01368 9

This fourth edition is dedicated in loving memory of my parents, Charles and Goldie Lewis. The memory of their dedication, guidance, and concern for my life and the lives of so many others is reflected in the pages of this book and in the hearts of families of soldiers everywhere.

Copyright © 2015 by Stackpole Books

First edition published 1998. Fourth edition 2015.

Published by
STACKPOLE BOOKS
5067 Ritter Road
Mechanicsburg, PA 17055
www.stackpolebooks.com

This book is not an official publication of the Department of Defense or Department of the Army, nor does its publication in any way imply its endorsement by these agencies. The views presented are those of the author and do not necessarily represent the views of the Department of Defense or its Components.

Printed in the United States of America

10 9 8 7 6 5 4 3 2 1

FOURTH EDITION

Cover design by Tessa Sweigert
Cover photo courtesy of the US Department of Defense
Use of military imagery does not imply or constitute endorsement of Stackpole Books, its products, or services by the US Department of Defense.

Library of Congress Cataloging-in-Publication Data

Lewis, Audie G.
    Career progression guide for soldiers : a practical guide for getting ahead in today's competitive Army / Audie G. Lewis. — Fourth edition.
        pages cm
    Includes index.
    ISBN 978-0-8117-1368-9
    1. United States. Army—Promotions.   2. United States. Army—Vocational guidance.   I. Title.
UB323.L43 2015
355.0023'73—dc23
                                                            2015002074

Contents

PART I: THE ENLISTED PROMOTION SYSTEM

Why the Army Promotes
The Decentralized Promotion System for Private through
    Specialist/Corporal
Special Advancements
Starting Off on the Right Foot
Duty Performance Is the Key to Success
An Example of a Soldier Who Excels
Strive for Secondary Zone Promotions
Additional Methods of Improving Skills
Avoiding the Pitfalls of Youth
Wiping the Slate Clean
Other Ways to Stand Out in the Crowd

A New Level of Responsibility
Primary and Secondary Zones of Consideration
Semicentralized Promotion System for Sergeants and Staff Sergeants
Promotion Point Reevaluations

The Highest Level of NCO Responsibility
Primary and Secondary Zones of Consideration
Typical Organization of a Centralized Board
Preparation: The Key to Success
Centralized Board Proceedings
Understanding Board Results
Factors in Secondary Zone Promotions

PART II: THE ROLE OF EDUCATION

PART III: PROGRESSION TO THE OFFICER RANKS

8   Commissioned Officer Selection 95
ROTC
West Point and West Point Prep School
OCS
Goarmy.com Green-to-Gold Program Access

PART IV: DEMONSTRATED TECHNIQUES
FOR PROMOTION AND COLLEGE

9   Sergeant Smith Gets Promoted 111
A Career Progression Interview with the Commander
Duty Performance and Board Points
Physical Training Improvement
Marksmanship Improvement
Awards Improvement
Military Education Improvement
Civilian Education Promotion Points through Testing
Sergeant Smith's Progress

10   Sergeant Jones Goes to College 127
Using an AARTS Transcript Effectively
Sergeant Jones Visits His College Advisor
The College Evaluates Sergeant Jones's Credit
Sergeant Jones Revisits His College Advisor
Sergeant Jones Registers for His First Class
Sergeant Jones's College Successes

PART V: SPECIAL TOPICS

11   Overcoming Major Career Progression Problems 135
QMP
RCP

12   Why Set Goals? 147
A New Soldier Takes Charge of His Career
Study Tests and Other Tools for Help with Goals

**13   Special Advice for Anyone Considering
Joining the Army** 157
Why the Military is an Excellent Career Choice
Promotion Pointers before You Join
The Extra Value of Military Experience

Acknowledgments

I am so grateful for all the wonderful assistance and patient encouragement received from Brittany Stoner at Stackpole Books. Her dedication and commitment to this fourth edition was a tremendous help and reflects strongly on the professionalism and excellence of the entire staff at Stackpole and the publishing world. I would also like to thank Kyle Weaver for his help with this important work.

Preface

The purpose of this book is to provide you with the tools necessary to manage your own military career progression and professional development. To a large extent, you are the master of your career. Your motivation (or lack thereof) to excel will determine the jobs you hold and the rank you will attain in the future. Unfortunately for most soldiers, very little information on or assistance with career management and progression is available at the unit level. It usually takes years of Army experience before a soldier can somewhat effectively manage his or her career. At that point, it often becomes obvious that a lack of knowledge has cost a soldier dearly. This guide can aid the soldier at every step of professional development and career progression.

You can benefit from this guide regardless of rank. For the young soldier, you will be more prepared to guide your career successfully from the start if you read and apply the ideas presented here rather than simply arriving at your first duty station and winging it. This book can help even new privates make a positive start in their Army careers. While most PV1s are promoted within six months, few realize that they can manage their careers to allow them to become promoted in only four months. And even more exciting is the possibility of making the rank of E-5 within two years of entering the Army! Even if being promoted at rocket speed is not your goal, this book should be indispensable to managing your early Army career.

This book will be especially helpful to soldiers who want to build points for promotion boards to the ranks of E-5 and E-6. Tips for increasing your promotion points in all possible areas are thoroughly discussed. Additionally, advice is given on facing the sometimes intimidating process of entering college and on making the most of a college program.

For those wishing to obtain the higher NCO ranks, or even for those striving to become a warrant or commissioned officer, this book will guide you through the various requirements and provide you with the best resources for reaching your goals as a professional soldier. If your career is being restrained due to past or present problems, such as a bad Noncommissioned Officer Evaluation Report (NCOER) or a qualitative management program (QMP) board decision, advice is given on how to manage your career despite these setbacks.

Officers will also benefit from reading this book. Functioning well within the Army should include a thorough understanding of the promotion system for all ranks, including the enlisted ranks. Commanders and leaders who truly want to implement sound promotion policies will do well to know how the system works and should be able to assist or point out to their soldiers any opportunities for professional development and promotion. This guide provides a wealth of material to aid in this soldier-care function.

Today's soldiers have countless opportunities to set and reach their professional goals. The *Career Progression Guide for Soldiers* can help any soldier in his or her attempt to reach those goals. All that is needed are self-motivation, a good plan, and the resources to make it happen. The resources exist and, for the most part, are free of charge.

Many things have changed since the first edition of the *Career Progression Guide for Soldiers* was published in 1998. Perhaps one of the biggest changes has been the rapid adoption and expansion of electronic communications within the military. Now more than ever, the Army is taking advantage of every conceivable form of electronic media in an effort to curb costs, increase efficiencies, and speed up processes. Army regulations, DA pamphlets, and a host of common forms are now available only as electronic publications and through digital repositories.

Likewise, college is available to more and more people regardless of their location or deployment status as a result of the eArmyU program, which allows soldiers to attend fully accredited and free "virtual" classes. Expectations have changed as well. Education is more important than ever to this rapidly changing modern Army. Promotions and success in today's Army increasingly hinge on the amount and quality of each soldier's civilian and military training arsenal. Rapid promotions definitely favor those with solid skills built through college coursework and enhanced military training. It could easily be argued that in today's Army promotions come quickest to those who have done their homework.

Part of that homework requirement could very well be additional foreign-language skills picked up from programs offered through the Defense Language Institute in Monterey, California. But don't pack your bags just yet, because most of these skills can be gained through the institute's online Learning Content Management System (LCMS), which is part of the overall Joint Knowledge Online (JKO) program.

Soldiers can earn a wealth of promotion points through the Headstart2 program, which includes a wide variety of languages available to be learned through either a downloadable program or a direct port to the DLI. It is a unique skill-learning site, one built specifically for aiding in many of today's soldier deployment tasks such as public safety, intelligence gathering, cordon-and-search, and medical missions.

This fourth edition of the *Career Progression Guide for Soldiers* incorporates the latest changes to Army regulations and programs while maintaining the timeless advice that has helped numerous others obtain greater success in reaching their goals. Additionally, this edition contains many of the newest website addresses and contact information needed to access the information and resources critical to a soldier's career progression.

Introduction

The increasing frequency and duration of unit deployments within recent years has placed a major strain on the armed services' ability to handle promotion, education, and career development pathways. Fortunately, the Army has responded to these changes with an ever-increasing move toward decentralized decision-making regarding promotions and related opportunities. The Department of the Army and Human Resource Command have delegated a wide degree of approvals downward toward the brigade and battalion command levels in an effort to improve the timeliness of these critically important soldier-care issues.

These changes will undoubtedly help soldiers be promoted more predictably and allow more of the emphasis on corrections and timeliness to be controlled by the individual as opposed to system administrators. Many routine tasks are now mandated as online-only submissions in order to streamline the Army's paperwork trails. Noncommissioned officer reports (NCOERs) are one of the many formerly paper-heavy functions that have been successfully automated.

The current environment for promotion and advancement is extremely good. Opportunities to get promoted faster or be selected for advanced training and/or commissioning sources are prevalent and attainable. Without a doubt, career advancement within the Army is more achievable than ever before!

One of the most significant changes in recent promotion activity is the increased value of military training. Although college education is still a critical component of the promotion system, the Army has shifted its emphasis to place more weight on mission-related aspects. These points of emphasis include military training that pushes soldiers to be more focused on education directly benefiting the unit mission and awards reflecting that same type of military commitment.

Changes have also included establishing a more direct correlation between correspondence training and unit mission. Soldiers must complete entire courses to obtain credit for this type of training. Completing individual booklets and topics no longer merits promotion credit under these system changes.

PART I

The Enlisted Promotion System

1

Promotions from Private through Specialist/Corporal

WHY THE ARMY PROMOTES

The Army promotes soldiers because it needs to. Although not necessarily profound, this statement does get to the heart of a very important Army function. Promotions happen because they are meant to fulfill specific Army objectives. Soldiers fill certain required jobs within the force structure of the Army. Each of these positions has various requirements for differing levels of responsibility, experience, and knowledge. These Army objectives are the keys to understanding the entire process and developing personal strategies that will enhance your potential for future success within this structure.

The Army promotes to fill authorized enlisted and officer spaces with qualified soldiers who have demonstrated an ability to perform at the next higher level. Promotions are also an important aspect of attracting and retaining high-caliber soldiers. The Army's goal is to keep the best soldiers and eliminate unproductive ones. Dedication, motivation, integrity, loyalty, and self-discipline are some of the attributes of a professional soldier that the Army looks for in selecting personnel for promotion or advancement. There are several avenues that the Army uses to find and select soldiers with these demonstrated qualities.

THE DECENTRALIZED PROMOTION SYSTEM FOR PRIVATE THROUGH SPECIALIST/CORPORAL

The majority of the promotion authority for the first level of the Army's promotion system rests with individual commanders of batteries, companies, and troops. They decide who should get promoted and the rate of promotion for the individual soldiers assigned or attached to their units. The Department of the Army still exercises some control over the process through regulated guidance such as minimum time-in-service (TIS) requirements, minimum time-in-grade (TIG) requirements, maximum waiver authority, and percentile limitations on soldiers that can be granted early promotions.

The Department of the Army also has set in place normal advancement time frames whereby promotion to the first three ranks takes place on designated anniversary months unless prevented by the local unit commander. Normally privates would advance to E-2 after six months of active federal service (AFS). PV2s advance to private first class (PFC) after twelve months of service and at least four months' time in grade. Likewise, PFCs would advance to the ranks of specialist (SPC) or corporal (CPL) after completing twenty-four months in service with six months' time in grade.

Normal time-in-service and time-in-grade promotions are known as *primary zone promotions*. Early promotions that require TIS or TIG waivers by the unit commander are known as *secondary zone promotions* and are reserved for the top soldiers within a unit. The unit commander can usually waive up to two months of TIS for advancement to PV2, provided that not more than 20 percent of his assigned and attached E-2 strength have less than six months' time in service.

Unit PFCs can receive waivers of up to six months of TIS and two months of TIG, as long as not more than 20 percent of the E-3 unit assigned and attached strength have less than twelve months' time in service. Waiver authority for E-4s is limited to three months' time in grade and fourteen months' time in service. These accelerated promotions to E-4 cannot allow more than 10 percent of the assigned and attached strength in the unit to have less than twenty-four months' time in service. The above rules are often tightened even further by periodic special messages from the Department of the Army.

Primary Zone Promotions	Secondary Zone Promotions
Promotion to PV2 at 6 months' TIS	Promotion to PV2 at 4 months' TIS
Promotion to PFC at 12 months' TIS	Promotion to PFC at 6 months' TIS
Promotion to SPC at 24 months' TIS	Promotion to SPC at 18 months' TIS

SPECIAL ADVANCEMENTS

There are some instances in which soldiers can be advanced to the next enlisted grade under special conditions. Three percent of basic training soldiers can be advanced to PV2 for outstanding performance without regard to time-in-service requirements. Some initial-entry contracts also allow for special advancement procedures based on the recruiting efforts of enlisting soldiers. Sometimes units will have unused waiver authorizations for promotions to E-4, which can be turned back to the next higher unit to be redistributed to other soldiers within the command.

The Army also periodically adjusts enlisted ranks for college education levels and certain other skills held by new enlistees. This is known as the Army and Army Reserve Civilian Acquired Skills Program (ACASP/ARCASP). Not only can new Army recruits begin their careers as E-3s, it is also possible for soldiers to be advanced to the rank of E-4 or E-5 on demonstrated ability and with a commander's recommendation.

Soldiers who do well on the Defense Language Aptitude Battery (DLAB) can acquire language training, which is an "MOS-enabler" skill, primarily in the electronic warfare/signal intelligence field. Selection includes language training at the Defense Language Institute-Foreign Language Center (DLI-FLC), located in the Presidio of Monterey, California. Courses last from twenty-five to forty-seven weeks, depending on the language. This can also be accessed through the Army e-Learning site, www.usarmy.skillport.com.

A good way to be advanced from E-1 to E-2 is by referring another person to the Army. By referring a qualified nonprior service applicant who enlists in the Delayed Entry Program, Active Army, Army National Guard, or US Army Reserve, an E-1 may be advanced to the rank of E-2.

STARTING OFF ON THE RIGHT FOOT

The old adage "You never get a second chance to make a good first impression" is especially true for soldiers arriving at their new units. Whether you're a brand-new private or a seasoned soldier, the impact of a first impression should not be underestimated. This is particularly important for new soldiers, since they do not have a documented work history. Once privates graduate from basic training and advanced individual training, they proceed immediately to their first duty assignment, where the commander and other unit leaders will make an initial judgment to determine soldier potential.

Most leaders look for several fundamental characteristics in new soldiers that help distinguish between an average soldier and an excellent soldier. These include a strong work ethic, good military discipline and bearing, sharp attention to military courtesy, personal initiative, and a positive attitude. Soldiers who concentrate on the development of these key traits tend to stand out from the crowd and are most often selected for early promotion.

These attributes can be strengthened through practice and good attention to detail. Many soldiers struggle with military courtesy, for example, and often may appear disrespectful or uninterested. Lack of respect may be acceptable in society, but it has no place in the military. Do not hesitate to show respect whenever it is in order, or even when it might not be in order. It is better to be cautious than to be taken as disrespectful. Soldiers who render sharp salutes and concentrate on conducting respectful communications generate mutual respect between the superior officer or noncommissioned officer and the new soldier. These courtesies are required by military regulation and should be performed wholeheartedly. It is definitely in your best interest to appear motivated in each of these required exchanges.

Personal appearance plays an important role as well. The military is a time-honored profession that demands personal sacrifice and commitment. Your uniform and appearance are visible indicators of the commitment you have to the military profession. Wear the uniform with pride, and ensure that it represents the best "you" that can be shown.

A good work ethic is essential for success in the military. Nothing is more damaging to a career than the reputation of being a lazy soldier. Instead, strive to do the best you can at all tasks given. Great effort and talent cannot be hidden. The most uninteresting job in the world can be used to demonstrate a positive work ethic and solid character. This is where a good attitude and personal initiative come together. Always seek to do every job to a high standard of excellence, and do not become satisfied with minimum standards. To stand out, a soldier needs to seek ways to exceed the expectations of his or her supervisor. Identify the experts, ask questions, and learn from them. Observe those who have earned the respect of the unit leaders, and pattern your work ethic and behavior after these successful soldiers.

DUTY PERFORMANCE IS THE KEY TO SUCCESS

Individual duty performance is the key to success in the Army, regardless of rank. Whether you are a private or a general, this truth remains constant. Your level of responsibility and scope of duties will change with each rank, but truly successful soldiers are dedicated to excellence in mission accomplishment. This commitment should include MOS skill competencies and proficiency in battle-focused training. Duty performance for lower enlisted soldiers (E-1 through E-4) is measured and recorded on a Developmental Counseling Form.

Another highly important part of a soldier's duty performance is commitment to excellence in physical fitness. Commit yourself to a strong, well-rounded program of maintaining or improving your physical fitness. It's not difficult to spot the high achievers in this area, and befriending them and asking them for advice is a good way to help achieve your physical fitness goals. Almost every installation has several excellent facilities and instructors or trainers to aid in your improvement. Establishing strength in this area is vitally important to your career if you intend to be a high achiever.

AN EXAMPLE OF A SOLDIER WHO EXCELS

Here's an example of a new private who takes all of the above advice and profits by implementing it.

Private Smith arrives at his unit and is assigned a five-ton truck with the responsibility for its maintenance and regular upkeep. He conducts his initial preventative maintenance checks and services (PMCS) of his vehicle and discovers that the truck is in very poor condition. He observes the other trucks in his section and realizes that most of his peers' vehicles are in similarly bad shape and that this seems to be the accepted standard within his section.

DEVELOPMENTAL COUNSELING FORM
For use of this form, see FM 6-22; the proponent agency is TRADOC.

DATA REQUIRED BY THE PRIVACY ACT OF 1974

PART I - ADMINISTRATIVE DATA

Name *(Last, First, MI)*	Rank/Grade	Date of Counseling
Organization	Name and Title of Counselor	

PART II - BACKGROUND INFORMATION

Purpose of Counseling: *(Leader states the reason for the counseling, e.g. Performance/Professional or Event-Oriented counseling, and includes the leader's facts and observations prior to the counseling.)*

PART III - SUMMARY OF COUNSELING
Complete this section during or immediately subsequent to counseling.

Key Points of Discussion:

OTHER INSTRUCTIONS
This form will be destroyed upon: reassignment *(other than rehabilitative transfers)* , separation at ETS, or upon retirement. For separation requirements and notification of loss of benefits/consequences see local directives and AR 635-200.

DA FORM 4856, AUG 2010   PREVIOUS EDITIONS ARE OBSOLETE.   APD LC v1.01ES

Developmental Counseling Form

Plan of Action *(Outlines actions that the subordinate will do after the counseling session to reach the agreed upon goal(s). The actions must be specific enough to modify or maintain the subordinate's behavior and include a specified time line for implementation and assessment (Part IV below)*

Session Closing: *(The leader summarizes the key points of the session and checks if the subordinate understands the plan of action. The subordinate agrees/disagrees and provides remarks if appropriate.)*

Individual counseled: ☐ I agree ☐ disagree with the information above.
Individual counseled remarks:

Signature of Individual Counseled: _____ Date: _____

Leader Responsibilities: *(Leader's responsibilities in implementing the plan of action.)*

Signature of Counselor: _____ Date: _____

PART IV - ASSESSMENT OF THE PLAN OF ACTION

Assessment: *(Did the plan of action achieve the desired results? This section is completed by both the leader and the individual counseled and provides useful information for follow-up counseling.)*

Counselor: _____ Individual Counseled: _____ Date of Assessment: _____

Note: Both the counselor and the individual counseled should retain a record of the counseling.

Developmental Counseling Form *continued*

Private Smith wishes to excel, so he starts putting in extra hours every day to improve the condition of his truck. After about a month, Private Smith's vehicle begins to get attention from higher-level leaders in the command because his truck stands out from the rest.

Private Smith begins to receive positive recognition from his unit commander and first sergeant, who see that he has high standards of performance. His uniform and appearance are above standard, his barracks room is spotless, he excels in physical training, and he always crisply salutes the commander and other unit officers.

A few weeks later, the commander is reviewing the monthly promotion roster and decides to promote Private Smith to PV2 two months early, even though there are others in the unit with more time in service. Private Smith soon becomes SPC Smith. The battery commander moves Specialist Smith to the unit orderly room as a unit clerk. His duty performance continues to be of high caliber, and a few months later he is sent to the promotion board to compete in the secondary zone of promotion to sergeant.

This scenario is not at all unrealistic. Too many soldiers are simply satisfied to be average performers. Most accept the status quo of their peers and never separate themselves in any way from the pack. Therefore, soldiers like Smith get noticed. It is rare for a motivated and dedicated soldier to be overlooked. If you are determined to be a top performer, then look for creative ways to separate yourself from the crowd. You will benefit greatly in the long run.

STRIVE FOR SECONDARY ZONE PROMOTIONS

You've read about the importance of your individual duty performance to your overall success as a soldier. Soldiers generally do not get promoted early because they fail to prepare properly for advancement. Excellent duty performance is key to promotions through E-4 because the unit commander decides which of his or her soldiers will be given the allotted slots for promotion. The commander also has approval authority to send soldiers to the local E-5 and E-6 boards. These decisions are almost always based totally on duty performance.

Duty performance will only partially prepare you for the actual promotion to the first NCO rank. You could be the best E-4 in the world and be recognized by your commander as such. You can be sent to the E-5 board at sixteen months of service (minimum time), but getting to the board early does not guarantee a secondary zone promotion to E-5. Most soldiers are on the promotion point standing lists for many months, and even years, before getting promoted to the next rank. This normally happens because they have not taken all available steps to getting promoted quickly.

ADDITIONAL METHODS OF IMPROVING SKILLS

There are additional methods of improving your skills that will help you in your early career and will benefit you even more later on. One such way is to begin your college education as soon as possible (Chapter 5 will get you started). Another method for advancement is to enroll in military training courses, such as correspondence courses in subjects that enhance your military skills. Your installation may also have local training courses, such as Nuclear, Biological, and Chemical (NBC) training or Small Arms Repair training, which aid the unit and develop individual soldier skills. These courses can later be used for promotion points to higher ranks. Additionally, soldiers who excel are more likely to receive unit awards and other forms of recognition, and such recognition increases the chances for secondary zone promotions.

Make sure you commit to all of the additional after-duty activities necessary to compete for future promotions while you are still a private. If you start this process as a private, then when secondary zone opportunities present themselves, you will have taken the necessary steps to get promoted quickly. You may even find yourself in a position to be chosen to compete for the training necessary to become a warrant or commissioned officer.

AVOIDING THE PITFALLS OF YOUTH

It is amazing the number of soldiers who get themselves in trouble over trivial issues. They decide to go out on the town and party with their friends and then chance driving home under the influence of alcohol, even though they know that their unit has a designated driver or similar program. Soldiers often ignore simple, yet important, aspects of military discipline, such as arriving to work on time or properly clearing appointments with their supervisors. These types of infractions may have seemed unimportant when in high school or at home under parental rules, but they can have grave consequences on a beginning military career. Preventive measures are the best prescription for long-term success. If you have trouble getting up on your own, then do something constructive to prevent problems. Owning more than one alarm clock is not unheard of. Try to be wise beyond your years to prevent problems and to establish a good reputation with your command and peers.

WIPING THE SLATE CLEAN

What if you have already gone over the line and gotten into trouble? Though it's not the ideal situation, these problems should not affect you in the long term if you are on your first enlistment. Article 15s for first-term soldiers are not filed in your permanent official military personnel file (OMPF). It may have a negative effect on you while you're in your current unit, but it need not follow you to subsequent assignments.

The best course is to put the bad incident behind you and to demonstrate your improved attitude and behavior to your leaders. It is imperative that you prove to your commander from the onset that you fully intend to move on. Also, take whatever punishment is given to you and execute your part wholeheartedly. If you are given extra duty, then try your best to give more than is required during the disciplinary period. Show up early for your additional duty, and even ask for additional tasks once the assigned ones are over. You may shock your supervisors with your remarkable attitude and have the unit commander talking about you in a positive rather than negative light.

An Article 15 violation, or similar disciplinary or retraining period, should not prevent you from having a good career. Handled correctly, it should only be a temporary setback to your long-term career goals. If you are a second-termer or have had more than one offense, you will have to address these issues at a later date. If you are applying for a warrant or commission, you will have to ask for a moral waiver (see Chapter 7 for an example). Otherwise, you should attempt to get the Article 15 moved to your restricted fiche as soon as possible (see the sample letter in Chapter 11). An Article 15 in your military record will probably not have any real effect on your potential for promotion until you compete for SFC and higher grades. By then, enough time should have passed that the Article 15 can be moved to your restricted fiche or removed from your file altogether.

OTHER WAYS TO STAND OUT IN THE CROWD
Everyone has individual skills and talents that often remain untapped because the normal duty day does not require these special skills. An example of this may be carpentry or other specialized talents that were acquired prior to entering the Army. You may be holding a job that has nothing to do with these abilities. Keep your eyes open for opportunities to use your skills. Whatever your talent or background, find your niche and make yourself indispensable to the unit. Your achievements will pave the way for future long-term success.

Individual and unit deployment readiness is one of the keys to success in today's Army. One of the components of that success in a global deployment environment is the need for soldiers with broad foreign language skills. The military recognizes this need and awards promotion credit and promotes individuals with skill sets that meet these requirements.

Young soldiers often have more time available to work on their career than they might have once they've gained more rank, experience, and time in service. Some of that extra time could be used to gain additional basic language skills that are important to future promotions. One of the ways to make yourself indispensable to the unit is to sign up for the Army Training Requirements and Resources System, which allows you access to programs for basic language skill subsets.

Many of the military's language skill requirements are met simply by learning key components of multiple languages, such as mastering important mission terms and phrases, performing writing drills, and undergoing animated military scenario learning, all of which teach the basics required for many of the duties and responsibilities of future jobs and deployment possibilities.

These skills can be learned in the comfort of your barracks room or home environment and even learned while engaged on a military exercise. The promotion points earned can be significant boosters to your military record and help distinguish you from other soldiers competing for special assignments, positions, and training.

2

Promotions to Sergeant and Staff Sergeant

A NEW LEVEL OF RESPONSIBILITY

Each promotion within the Army force structure demands an increased level of responsibility and requires an even greater degree of professional service. Noncommissioned officers play a very important role in this process. NCOs are expected to set and enforce standards, provide professional leadership, and train their soldiers. They need a strong educational base and a competent array of skills in order to function confidently and decisively. Noncommissioned officers also have an important role in making sure the Army is ready for combat. They must be tactically and technically proficient in their duties and ensure that each of their soldiers is equally proficient.

PRIMARY AND SECONDARY ZONES OF CONSIDERATION

Normal time-in-service (TIS) and time-in-grade (TIG) promotions are known as primary zone promotions. Early promotions that require TIS or TIG waivers by the unit commander are known as secondary zone promotions. The top performers in a unit are normally chosen to compete in the secondary zone of consideration.

The primary zone of consideration for promotion to E-5 begins at thirty-six months of active federal service (AFS) with at least eight months' time in grade as an E-4. Secondary zone promotions allow for this TIS and TIG requirement to be cut in half. Each of these semicentralized promotions requires a sixty-day delay between board attendance and actual promotion to the next grade. It is conceivable that a soldier could attend the E-5 promotion board as early as sixteen months of AFS and be promoted two months later with only eighteen months of total active federal service.

The primary zone of consideration for E-6 begins at eighty-four months of active federal service with at least ten months of time in grade as an E-5. The TIS requirement can be reduced to forty-eight months and the TIG requirement cut in half to allow for a secondary zone of promotion with only forty-eight months of total TIS (if the soldier was boarded at forty-six months' time in service).

PROMOTION POINT WORKSHEET For use of this form, see AR 600-8-19; the proponent agency is DCS, G-1.	1. TYPE ☐ a. Initial ☐ b. Total Reevaluation	2. DATE *(YYYYMMDD)*

DATA REQUIRED BY THE PRIVACY ACT OF 1974

AUTHORITY:	Title 5 USC, Section 301.
PRINCIPAL PURPOSE:	To determine eligibility for promotion.
ROUTINE USES:	Reviewed to determine promotion eligibility and validity of points granted.
DISCLOSURE:	The furnishing of fraudulent information may result in denial of promotion.

3. NAME	4. RECOMMENDED GRADE
5. ORGANIZATION	6. PMOS

SECTION A - RECOMMENDATION

1. MILITARY TRAINING *(Maximum 100 Points)*

a. LATEST APFT DATE *(YYYYMMDD)*	b. SCORES				c. POINTS AWARDED
	PUSH-UPS	SIT-UPS	RUN	TOTAL	

d. LATEST WEAPONS QUALIFICATION DATE *(YYYYMMDD)*	e. DA FORM USED:	f. TOTAL HITS	g. POINTS AWARDED

h. TOTAL POINTS AWARDED ————————————————➤	

2. DUTY PERFORMANCE EVALUATION *(Maximum 150 Points Award 1-30 Points For Each Category)*

CATEGORY	POINTS AWARDED
a. COMPETENCE: Proficient, Knowledgeable, Communicates Effectively	
b. MILITARY BEARING: Role Model, Appearance, Confidence	
c. LEADERSHIP: Motivates Soldiers, Sets Standards, Mission, Concern	
d. TRAINING: Individual and Team, Shares Knowledge and Experience, Teaching	
e. RESPONSIBILITY AND ACCOUNTABILITY: Equipment, Facilities, Safety, Conservation	
f. TOTAL POINTS AWARDED ————————————————➤	

I certify that the above APFT and weapons qualification scores shown have been extracted from appropriate records and the latest valid scores are in accordance with Army Training Regulations and Army Field Manuals.

3. SIGNATURE OF COMMANDER	4. TYPED OR PRINTED NAME AND GRADE	5. DATE *(YYYYMMDD)*

SECTION B - ADMINISTRATIVE POINTS

1. AWARDS, DECORATIONS AND ACHIEVEMENTS *(Maximum 100 Points. List all awards individually. Include award number (i.e. 3rd OLC) and the order number.)*

TOTAL POINTS AWARDED ————————————————➤	

DA FORM 3355, APR 2010   PREVIOUS EDITIONS ARE OBSOLETE.

Promotion Point Worksheet

NAME

2. MILITARY EDUCATION *(Maximum 200 Points. List all military education.)*

TOTAL POINTS AWARDED →

3. CIVILIAN EDUCATION *(Maximum 100 Points. List all civilian education.)*

TOTAL POINTS AWARDED →

I certify that the above administrative points shown have been accurately extracted from appropriate records and that the promotion points indicated are correct.

4. TYPED OR PRINTED NAME OF RESPONSIBLE OFFICIAL	5. DATE *(YYYYMMDD)*	6. SIGNATURE OF RECOMMENDED INDIVIDUAL *(Required)*	7. DATE *(YYYYMMDD)*

SECTION C - TOTALS

Only whole numbers will be used in awarding promotion points for all sections (drop fractions). Only initial and total reevaluations require submission of DA From 3355. Administrative reevaluations and adjustments are submitted on DA Form 4187 and annotated in the Eval/Adj column.

1. POINTS GRANTED

ITEM	INITIAL *(Date)*	EVAL/ADJ *(Date)*	EVAL/ADJ *(Date)*	EVAL/ADJ *(Date)*	EVAL/ADJ *(Date)*	EVAL/ADJ *(Date)*
a. TOTAL PERFORMANCE EVALUATION AND MILITARY TRAINING POINTS - SECTION A *(Maximum 250 points)*						
b. TOTAL ADMINISTRATIVE POINTS - SECTION B *(Maximum 400 points)*						
c. TOTAL BOARD POINTS *(Maximum 150 points)*						
d. TOTAL PROMOTION POINTS *(Maximum 800 points)*						
2. INITIALS OF RESPONSIBLE PSB OFFICIAL						

SECTION D - CERTIFICATION

I certify that the above total points shown have been accurately extracted from appropriate records and promotion list points indicated are correct.

1. RECOMMENDED BY BOARD ☐ YES ☐ NO	2. ATTAINED MINIMUM POINTS ☐ YES ☐ NO		
3. TYPED OR PRINTED NAME AND SIGNATURE OF BOARD RECORDER	4. GRADE	5. DATE *(YYYYMMDD)*	

I certify that the soldier has been recommended for promotion by a valid promotion board.

6. TYPED OR PRINTED NAME OF PROMOTION AUTHORITY	7. SIGNATURE	8. DATE PROCEEDINGS WERE APPROVED *(YYYYMMDD)*

Counseling statement: I have been counseled on my promotion status and deficiencies. *(Use only when recommendation is disapproved, when a soldier is not selected by a board, or when a soldier cannot be added to the recommended list due to not attaining the minimum required points).*

9. SIGNATURE OF SOLDIER	10. DATE *(YYYYMMDD)*	11. TYPED OR PRINTED NAME AND SIGNATURE OF COUNSELOR

Promotion Point Worksheet *continued*

Primary Zone Promotions	**Secondary Zone Promotions**
Promotion to SGT at 36 months' TIS	Promotion to SGT at 18 months' TIS
Promotion to SSG at 84 months' TIS	Promotion to SSG at 48 months' TIS
Promotions are not automatic	*Based on board appearance 2 months prior*

SEMICENTRALIZED PROMOTION SYSTEM FOR SERGEANTS AND STAFF SERGEANTS

Promotions for sergeants and staff sergeants are semicentralized and based on an 800-point system. The Army considers these promotions semicentralized because the promotion authority is divided between unit commanders and the Department of the Army. Promotion boards are normally conducted at the battalion level with board members from the senior NCO ranks within the unit.

The Department of the Army sets the promotion cutoff scores for each month. It uses these cutoff scores as a tool to manage promotions within each of the enlisted military occupational specialties (MOSs). The cutoff scores are periodically lowered to allow soldiers on the promotion standing lists to be promoted. The lower the score is dropped, the more people that are promoted. Overstrength MOSs normally have high cutoff scores and slow promotions, whereas understrength MOSs traditionally have low cutoff scores and faster promotions. All of the scores are achievable, including the seemingly impossible 798 cutoff score. This chapter will describe in detail each of the six separate areas of the promotion packet used for semicentralized promotions. Chapter 9 demonstrates practical methods for achieving higher scores by examining the sample packet of a hypothetical Army sergeant.

The Promotion Point Structure chart shows the breakdown of the promotion packet and sections used for these semicentralized promotions. This 800-point system is used for both E-5 and E-6 promotions. Although the total number of points for promotion to E-5 and E-6 remains the same, there have been significant changes in how the points are earned and used toward each section of these respective ranks. These changes reflect the Army's desire for a greater leadership portfolio for promotion to the E-6 rank. The points awarded also reflect differences in earned points for the Army Physical Fitness Test (APFT) and Weapons Qualifications related to these semicentralized promotions.

Duty Performance

Unit commanders decide who will be sent to the local promotion boards and also who is ready for integration into the existing promotion list (or no longer eligible). Under the new promotion system, commanders do not award promotion points.

The decision to promote under the semicentralized system will still be based on the commander's objective evaluation of the soldier's current and past duty performance. The most commonly used criteria for judging conduct expected of a noncommissioned officer are found on DA Form 2166-8-1, NCO/Counseling Checklist/Record, and the NCO Evaluation Report.

SGT PROMOTION POINT STRUCTURE

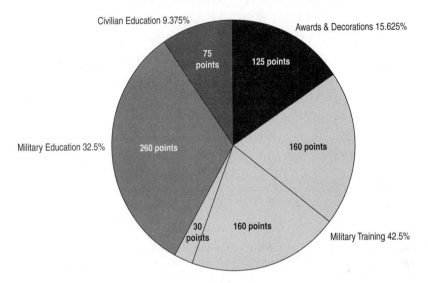

Civilian Education 9.375%

Awards & Decorations 15.625%

75 points

125 points

Military Education 32.5%

260 points

160 points

30 points

160 points

Military Training 42.5%

Although there are zero promotion points awarded for board and commander recommendation, each is still required—the commander still has to recommend you, and the promotion board now must give a "Go" or "No Go" validation to the recommendation.

SSG PROMOTION POINT STRUCTURE

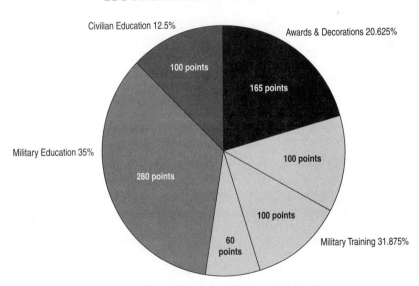

Civilian Education 12.5%

Awards & Decorations 20.625%

100 points

165 points

Military Education 35%

100 points

280 points

100 points

60 points

Military Training 31.875%

Although there are zero promotion points awarded for board and commander recommendation, each is still required—the commander still has to recommend you, and the promotion board now must give a "Go" or "No Go" validation to the recommendation.

SGT PROMOTION POINTS AVAILABLE & PERCENTAGES

Section Title	Possible Points	Percentage of Total
Awards & Decorations	125	15.625
Military Training:	340	42.5
Marksmanship	(160)	
Physical Readiness	(160)	
Deployment Experience	(30)	
Military Education	260	32.5
Civilian Education	75	9.375
Total:	800	100 percent

Note: Maxing Deployment Experience does not mean that the soldier can exceed the total point value allowed for Military Training. This is an overlapping benefit that can compensate for weakness in Physical Readiness or Marksmanship only. Max value of 30 points for SGT.

SSG PROMOTION POINTS AVAILABLE & PERCENTAGES

Section Title	Possible Points	Percentage of Total
Awards & Decorations	165	20.625
Military Training:	255	31.875
Marksmanship	(100)	
Physical Readiness	(100)	
Deployment Experience	(60)	
Military Education	280	35
Civilian Education	100	12.5
Total:	800	100 percent

Note: Maxing Deployment Experience does not mean that the soldier can exceed the total point value allowed for Military Training. This is an overlapping benefit that can compensate for weakness in Physical Readiness or Marksmanship only. Max value of 60 points for SSG.

NCOER COUNSELING AND SUPPORT FORM
For use of this form, see AR 623-3 ; the proponent agency is DCS, G-1.

PART I - ADMINISTRATIVE DATA

a. NAME *(Last, First, Middle Initial)*	b. SSN	c. RANK	d. DATE OF RANK	e. PMOSC

f. UNIT, ORG., STATION, ZIP CODE OR APO, MAJOR COMMAND	STATUS CODE	l. RATED NCO'S EMAIL ADDRESS *(.gov or .mil)*	m. UIC	n. CMD CODE	o. PSB CODE

PART II - AUTHENTICATION

a. NAME OF RATER *(Last, First, Middle Initial)*	SSN	INITIAL	LATER	LATER	LATER
RANK, PMOSC/BRANCH, ORGANIZATION, DUTY ASSIGNMENT		RATER'S AKO EMAIL ADDRESS *(.gov. or .mil)*			
b. NAME OF SENIOR RATER *(Last, First, Middle Initial)*	SSN	INITIAL	LATER	LATER	LATER
RANK, PMOSC/BRANCH, ORGANIZATION, DUTY ASSIGNMENT		SENIOR RATER'S AKO EMAIL ADDRESS *(.gov. or .mil)*			
c. NAME OF REVIEWER *(Last, First, Middle Initial)*	SSN	INITIAL	LATER	LATER	LATER
RANK, PMOSC/BRANCH, ORGANIZATION, DUTY ASSIGNMENT		REVIEWER'S AKO EMAIL ADDRESS *(.gov. or .mil)*			
d. RATED NCO's INITIAL's		INITIAL	LATER	LATER	LATER

PART III - DUTY DESCRIPTION *(Rater)*

a. PRINCIPAL DUTY TITLE	b. DUTY MOSC

c. DAILY DUTIES AND SCOPE *(To include, as appropriate, people, equipment, facilities and dollars)*

d. AREAS OF SPECIAL EMPHASIS

e. APPOINTED DUTIES

f. PHYSICAL FITNESS & MILITARY BEARING

    APFT   APFT DATE   HEIGHT/WEIGHT

PART IV - ARMY VALUES/ATTRIBUTES/SKILLS/ACTIONS *(Rater)*

a. ARMY VALUES:

LOYALTY, DUTY, RESPECT/EO/EEO, SELFLESS-SERVICE, HONOR, INTEGRITY, PERSONAL

TASK/ACTIONS: PERFORMANCE SUMMARY:

NCOER Counseling and Support Form

RATED NCO'S NAME (Last, First, Middle Initial)		SSN

b. COMPETENCE:
o Duty proficiency; MOS competency   o Technical & tactical; knowledge, skills, and abilities
o Sound judgment   o Seeking self-improvement; always learning
o Accomplishing tasks to the fullest capacity; committed to excellence

TASK/ACTIONS:	PERFORMANCE SUMMARY:

c. PHYSICAL FITNESS & MILITARY BEARING: o Mental and physical toughness   o Endurance and stamina to go the distance
o Displaying confidence and enthusiasm; looks like a soldier

TASK/ACTIONS:	PERFORMANCE SUMMARY:

d. LEADERSHIP:
o Mission first   o Genuine concern for soldiers
o Instilling the spirit to achieve and win   o Setting the example; Be, Know, Do

TASK/ACTIONS:	PERFORMANCE SUMMARY:

e. TRAINING:
o Individual and team   o Mission focused; performance oriented
o Teaching soldiers how; common tasks, duty-related skills   o Sharing knowledge and experience to fight, survive and win

TASK/ACTIONS:	PERFORMANCE SUMMARY:

f. RESPONSIBILITY & ACCOUNTABILITY:
o Care and maintenance of equipment/facilities   o Soldier and equipment safety
o Conservation of supplies and funds   o Encouraging soldiers to learn and grow
o Responsible for good, bad, right & wrong

TASK/ACTIONS:	PERFORMANCE SUMMARY:

DA FORM 2166-8-1, OCT 2011

NCOER Counseling and Support Form *continued*

The checklist and the NCOER are excellent tools used by many leaders because they identify standards of excellence expected of noncommissioned officers. The checklist is broken into six different areas covering important values and responsibilities. The areas covered are competence, physical fitness and military bearing, leadership, training, responsibility and accountability, and individual values. The checklist is a valuable tool for many leaders because it emphasizes measurable performance.

You should probably meet with your commander to discuss his or her evaluation of your duty performance, particularly if he or she has determined that you are not ready for promotion to the next rank. The meeting should be beneficial to you regardless of the outcome, because you will have identified areas in which you can improve your performance in the future.

Awards and Decorations

Awards represent special recognition for acts of heroism, valor, outstanding service or achievement, and particular skills that distinguish one soldier from another. In the promotion packet, these awards carry real weight in actual point value.

Points for individual awards vary by rank and category. For soldiers competing for promotion to E-5, this category is worth 125 points and valued at 15.625 percent of the total 800-point score. For soldiers competing for E-6, this award category is worth 165 points and represents 20.625 percent of the overall promotion point score. These changes represent major differences from the

LIST OF COMMON AWARDS WITH CURRENT POINT VALUE

Award	Points	Award	Points
Soldier's Medal	40	Drill Sergeant & Recruiter Badges	15
Combat Infantry Badge	30	Soldier/NCO of the Quarter—Inst/Div	15
Expert Medical Badge	30	Joint Service Achievement Medal	10
Bronze Star Medal	30	Good Conduct Medal	10
Purple Heart Medal	30	Driver & Mechanic Badges	10
Combat Medical Badge	30	Explosive Ordnance Badge	10
Expert Infantry Badge	30	Soldier/NCO of the Quarter—Bde	10
Defense Meritorious Service Medal	25	Ranger and Special Forces Tabs	10
Soldier/NCO of the Year—MACOM	25	Parachutist Badge	10
Meritorious Service Medal	25	Pathfinder or Diver's Badge	10
Joint Service Commendation Medal	20	Nuclear Reactor Operator Badge	5
Air Medal	20	Aircraft Crewman Badge	5
Army Commendation Medal	20	Certificates of Achievement	5
Army Achievement Medal	15	Southwest Asia Medal	3

previous semicentralized promotion system. The Army believes that awards are more representative of the actual duty performance of the soldier, and so they carry more weight in the new promotion system.

This area is often one of the weakest areas for newer soldiers, especially when competing for a secondary zone promotion. Soldiers often receive awards for periods of service to a unit when they make a permanent change-of-station (PCS) move. Soldiers with more time in service will generally have had more opportunities to receive awards.

This is not always true for high achievers, however. Many soldiers appear to routinely receive awards because they continuously outperform their peers. This is also often the case with special skill badges, because they represent awards that require completion of some type of training and testing. High achievers frequently search for and request opportunities to participate in these special skill badge-certification programs.

A Look at Some of the More Common Awards

Certificates of Achievement. Usually considered the easiest awards to get, because they are often given out for more generic acts of achievement. This is a common award to receive for participation in areas that received excellent ratings during annual inspections or similar events found within most military units. They are also often presented to soldiers for exceeding physical fitness standards set by unit commanders. These awards will count for promotion board points if they are signed by a lieutenant colonel, a brigade command sergeant major, or higher. These are excellent awards for any soldier, but only four total can be used in your promotion packet (20 points total).

Driver Badge. Awarded for a high degree of skill in the safe operation of a military vehicle. The soldier must have held a US government vehicle operator's license and been fully qualified to drive. The badge can be awarded to a soldier who has either driven 8,000 accident-free miles or had a safe driving record for a minimum of twelve consecutive months as either a driver or an assistant driver. The safe-driving requirement also means no recorded traffic violations within the mileage or time period covered. The badge can also be awarded to a soldier who performed as a qualified driver instructor or a special equipment operator for twelve consecutive months. The Driver Badge may be awarded by any commander in the grade of LTC or higher.

Mechanic Badge. Awarded to qualified unit mechanics when assigned as a mechanic and when required to operate motor vehicles in conjunction with assigned duties for at least six consecutive months. The soldier also must be properly licensed to drive and operate the equipment and have had no recorded traffic violations or vehicle accidents. The Mechanic Badge may be awarded by any commander in the grade of LTC or higher.

Expert Infantry Badge. Can be earned by any infantry soldier who competes for and passes the required proficiency tests. These tests are set up and administered within training regions where infantry units are normally located.

Expert Field Medical Badge. Can be earned by any member of the Army Medical Service upon successful competition of the required proficiency tests. Testing is administered within training regions where needed for the local Army medical community. Combat lifesavers are not eligible to compete for this badge.

Aviation Badge. Awarded to qualified crewmembers assigned duties within Army aviation units. Duties within aircraft determine eligibility and qualifications required.

Parachutist Badge. Awarded upon satisfactory completion of the Airborne School at Fort Benning, Georgia. Soldiers from almost every MOS are eligible to apply. Soldiers can request a slot through their Personnel Service Center. Statistically, most slots are given out to coincide with a regular permanent-change-of-station (PCS) move.

Airborne Advantage. Soldiers who have earned their Airborne wings receive additional points beyond the badge when serving in an authorized airborne position and receiving Hazardous Duty Incentive Pay (Parachute Duty Pay). The extra points are contingent on which badge level they hold and the associated duty position receiving the incentive. The following table shows the differentials between the three separate positions that are authorized additional promotion packet points while serving under these conditions.

HAZARDOUS DUTY AIRBORNE ADVANTAGE PROMOTION POINTS

Badge Level	Additional Promotion Point Value
Parachutist	20
Senior Parachutist	25
Master Parachutist	30

Air Assault Badge. Sometimes referred to as rappelling school, this course of instruction is presented either by one of several Training and Doctrine Command (TRADOC) schools or through the course taught by the 101st Air Assault Division at Fort Campbell, Kentucky. This course is also requested through the local Personnel Service Center.

Physical Fitness Training Badge. Awarded to soldiers who score at least 290 on the Army Physical Fitness Test (APFT). It can be awarded by any commander in the grade of LTC or higher. It is definitely worth the time to compete for this badge: A high score on the APFT carries additional weight in promotion points for the Physical Readiness Training portion of the promotion packet.

Army Achievement Medal. A medal very important to most soldiers because it is the only meritorious achievement or meritorious service medal that can be approved by the unit battalion commander. Soldiers often receive this award for exceptional performance of duty. This is the most likely reward given for outstanding personal achievement. There is no limit to how many of these awards can be counted for promotion packets. These awards are more likely to be approved, because the battalion commander often is very knowledgeable about the circumstances that warranted the recommendation.

Army Commendation Medal. This is the most common award given to soldiers for meritorious service when they leave a unit. It also is often used to reward exceptionally outstanding personal achievement. Commanders in the grade of colonel and above are the approval authority.

Soldier/NCO of the Quarter. Competitive wins within the arena of local area evaluation boards can provide soldiers with considerable additional promotion points, especially in brigade and higher competitions. Brigade-level recognition is worth 10 points. Success in installation or division-level competition raises the value to 15 points. MACOM-level attainment of Soldier/NCO of the Year is worth 25 points. Each of these competitions is well worth the effort in terms of professional performance and promotion potential.

Some Tips on Related Award Issues

Leaders at every level have considerable influence on what awards soldiers receive, yet soldiers will not receive awards that first-line supervisors forget to recommend. The unit commander has a limited knowledge of the quality and degree of work carried out by each man and woman under his or her command, and therefore it is imperative that soldier leaders make it a priority to recognize their people. It is also appropriate to suggest that your supervisor put you in for an award.

Some awards tend to get overlooked more than others, even though they may be easily obtained. Driver and Mechanic Badges are relatively easy to get if the unit is dedicated to the task of collecting and evaluating these sources. The battalion commander is also an important part of this equation. His or her signature is probably the most important one to younger soldiers, as he or she has the approval authority for Certificates of Achievement, Driver and Mechanic Badges, Physical Fitness Badges, and Army Achievement Medals. These four award areas make up the majority of all awards given. The best leaders learn to correctly spotlight their top performers so that they are adequately rewarded for a job well done.

An often overlooked category involves equivalent awards and decorations earned while serving in other military branches. There are plenty of Army soldiers who have completed periods of service in the US Air Force, Navy, Coast Guard, Army Reserve, National Guard, or Marines. Their records are sometimes hard to obtain, and doing so may require a concerted effort by the chain of command. Awards from the various military branches all carry comparative promotion points and only require verification and evaluation by the promotions section of the local Personnel Service Center.

Military Training Section and Marksmanship Improvement

The Army has drastically changed this promotion point section for soldiers competing for SGT and SSG within the semicentralized promotion system. The Army has also varied the number of points available to reflect the different levels of promotion. For instance, those competing for promotion to E-5 can receive up to 340 points, which represents a whopping 42.5 percent of the overall score for promotion to that rank. Soldier leaders competing for E-6 are also awarded more points than under the previous promotion system, but scores are limited to 255 points for SSG, which accounts for 31.8 percent of an overall promotion packet score.

Soldiers competing for promotion in this area can also gain additional points for deployment experience. They earn up to 2 points per month for a maximum of 15 months when competing for promotion to E-5 (30 points) and a maximum of 30 months when competing for promotions to E-6 (60 points). There are also different scales used for awarding promotion point credit for APFT and Weapons Qualification in each of the ranks and promotion categories. Please note the differences for each score shown in the two charts that follow for E-5 and E-6 promotions.

PROMOTION POINTS FOR MARKSMANSHIP
BASED ON FIRING RECORD FOR SGT

DA Form 3695 (M16)	DA Form 88 (Pistol)	MP Firearm Qualification Course
40 = 160	30 = 160	50 = 160
39 = 153	29 = 151	49 = 152
38 = 145	28 = 142	48 = 144
37 = 138	27 = 133	47 = 135
36 = 130	26 = 124	46 = 127
35 = 123	25 = 115	45 = 119
34 = 115	24 = 106	44 = 110
33 = 108	23 = 97	43 = 102
32 = 100	22 = 88	42 = 94
31 = 93	21 = 79	41 = 85
30 = 85	20 = 70	40 = 77
29 = 78	19 = 61	39 = 69
28 = 70	18 = 52	38 = 60
27 = 63	17 = 43	37 = 52
26 = 55	16 = 33	36 = 43
25 = 48		35 = 33
24 = 40		
23 = 33		

PROMOTION POINTS FOR MARKSMANSHIP
BASED ON FIRING RECORD FOR SSG

DA Form 3695 (M16)	DA Form 88 (Pistol)	MP Firearm Qualification Course
40 = 100	30 = 100	50 = 100
39 = 98	29 = 98	49 = 96
38 = 96	28 = 96	48 = 92
37 = 94	27 = 88	47 = 88
36 = 92	26 = 80	46 = 82
35 = 86	25 = 74	45 = 78
34 = 80	24 = 68	44 = 72
33 = 74	23 = 60	43 = 68
32 = 68	22 = 52	42 = 62
31 = 62	21 = 48	41 = 58
30 = 56	20 = 44	40 = 52
29 = 52	19 = 40	39 = 48
28 = 48	18 = 36	38 = 42
27 = 44	17 = 32	37 = 38
26 = 40	16 = 28	36 = 32
25 = 36		35 = 28
24 = 32		
23 = 28		

These are huge changes for today's soldiers. They represent the Army's commitment to tying more of the promotion authority directly to the actions of the individual soldiers and the local units. The military believes this area of the promotion packet is a better predictor of future top performance among soldiers. The Army has proven its commitment to this belief by awarding significant weight to these areas within the promotion packet.

This area of the promotion packet is often neglected, even though it is probably one of the easiest in which to gain points. A few hours of extra training here will definitely be worth the time invested. Most soldiers qualify as sharpshooter with little extra training conducted other than the experiential training received as part of the normal rifle range qualification process.

Marksmanship Training Tips. There are a lot of techniques that can be used to quickly master many of the skills necessary to improve marksmanship scores. Improper breathing is the most common problem associated with poor marksmanship. Soldiers are routinely told to breathe properly but often are not shown the techniques to acquire this skill. Professional marksmen often use a dime or washer drill to perfect breathing and steady hold factors. This technique involves putting a dime or washer on the barrel of the rifle and attempting to keep it in place while pulling the trigger.

To begin this exercise, the weapon is unloaded and precocked and given to the marksman in whatever stance is appropriate for the training, such as the prone or prone supported position. If the marksman pulls the trigger and the dime or washer falls off the barrel, the marksman repeats the trial until successful. Skills can be improved even further by changing the test slightly; one modification is inserting a standard cleaning rod inside the barrel and balancing the dime or washer on the end of the rod. (Do not use a flat extension on the rod.)

To correct poor sight picture, marksmen often use the shadowbox drill. This drill is used to train marksmen who have problems returning to the same sight picture that they previously used to engage a target. This is especially true for zero ranges. Soldiers who never correctly zero are unlikely to score well on a subsequent firing range. In this drill, a box that has a cutout for a paper card is used. The cutout is fashioned like a typical target sight picture so that the marksman should be able to align the weapon's sights on the box in the same manner as when engaging a standard target.

An assistant inserts a piece of paper in front of the cutout and holds it in place until the marksman tells him to mark the paper. The paper is removed and the process repeated until the marksman can routinely sight the pen dot to appear immediately around the other pen dots. This training drastically improves one's ability to continuously regain the previous sight picture. Shadowbox training aids are usually available through the local Training and Support Center (TASC).

Effective coaching is invaluable in improving marksmanship skills. This requires knowledgeable trainers that go through the qualification process with the firer and coach him or her through each of the ranges. The coach's job is to correct poor firing behavior as it actually occurs during the firing process. This is a very effective means of improving unit firing skills, so long as the coaches are well trained and routinely fire expertly themselves. This method is only as good as the coach, however.

Marksmanship improvement graphic training aids (GTA) are available by email request from teamgta@atsc.army.mil or by written correspondence to Training Media Support Team, Individual Training Support Directorate, Army Training Support Center, 1557 11th St., Fort Eustis, VA 23604.

Military Training Section and Physical Readiness Improvement

This area of the semicentralized promotion packet has also undergone changes from previous promotion programs. Like many of the other areas, the Army has separated the points awarded by grade and rank. For soldiers competing for promotion to E-5, the new APFT scores account for up to 20 percent of the overall packet score; this represents 160 points out of a possible 800 total. For soldiers competing for promotion to E-6, this area is now worth 100 points, which represents 12.5 percent of their overall packet score. This is a much greater weight than was previously given this section. The following chart shows the differences between the scores received for both SGT and SSG.

A soldier's physical condition is a very important aspect of his or her military career. Personal neglect in this area will certainly slow down your career and limit your usefulness to the military. On the other hand, excellence in this one area will increase your future possibilities for success in many areas.

PROMOTION POINTS FOR PHYSICAL FITNESS
BASED ON APFT RECORD (FOR SGT)

SCORE = POINTS	SCORE = POINTS	SCORE = POINTS	SCORE = POINTS
300 = 160	270 = 130	240 = 100	210 = 70
299 = 159	269 = 129	239 = 99	209 = 69
298 = 158	268 = 128	238 = 98	208 = 68
297 = 157	267 = 127	237 = 97	207 = 67
296 = 156	266 = 126	236 = 96	206 = 66
295 = 155	265 = 125	235 = 95	205 = 65
294 = 154	264 = 124	234 = 94	204 = 64
293 = 153	263 = 123	233 = 93	203 = 63
292 = 152	262 = 122	232 = 92	202 = 62
291 = 151	261 = 121	231 = 91	201 = 61
290 = 150	260 = 120	230 = 90	200 = 60
289 = 149	259 = 119	229 = 89	199 = 59
288 = 148	258 = 118	228 = 88	198 = 58
287 = 147	257 = 117	227 = 87	197 = 57
286 = 146	256 = 116	226 = 86	196 = 56
285 = 145	255 = 115	225 = 85	195 = 55
284 = 144	254 = 114	224 = 84	194 = 54
283 = 143	253 = 113	223 = 83	193 = 53
282 = 142	252 = 112	222 = 82	192 = 52
281 = 141	251 = 111	221 = 81	191 = 51
280 = 140	250 = 110	220 = 80	190 = 50
279 = 139	249 = 109	219 = 79	189 = 49
278 = 138	248 = 108	218 = 78	188 = 48
277 = 137	247 = 107	217 = 77	187 = 47
276 = 136	246 = 106	216 = 76	186 = 46
275 = 135	245 = 105	215 = 75	185 = 45
274 = 134	244 = 104	214 = 74	184 = 44
273 = 133	243 = 103	213 = 73	183 = 43
272 = 132	242 = 102	212 = 72	182 = 42
271 = 131	241 = 101	211 = 71	181 = 41
			180 = 40

There are many methods for improving your level of fitness. One of the most basic ways is to increase both the amount of time spent in training and the intensity of the training. For instance, it is well documented that doing lots of push-ups, sit-ups, and running will increase your ability to do better on these events. Many soldiers do other physical fitness and cardiovascular endurance exercises that also improve their overall ability to do well on these events. It

PROMOTION POINTS FOR PHYSICAL FITNESS
BASED ON APFT RECORD (FOR SSG)

SCORE = POINTS	SCORE = POINTS	SCORE = POINTS	SCORE = POINTS
300 = 100	270 = 75	240 = 45	210 = 28
299 = 99	269 = 74	239 = 44	209 = 28
298 = 99	268 = 73	238 = 43	208 = 27
297 = 98	267 = 72	237 = 42	207 = 27
296 = 98	266 = 71	236 = 41	206 = 26
295 = 97	265 = 70	235 = 41	205 = 26
294 = 97	264 = 69	234 = 40	204 = 25
293 = 96	263 = 68	233 = 40	203 = 25
292 = 96	262 = 67	232 = 39	202 = 24
291 = 95	261 = 66	231 = 39	201 = 24
290 = 95	260 = 65	230 = 38	200 = 23
289 = 94	259 = 64	229 = 38	199 = 23
288 = 93	258 = 63	228 = 37	198 = 22
287 = 92	257 = 62	227 = 37	197 = 22
286 = 91	256 = 61	226 = 36	196 = 21
285 = 90	255 = 60	225 = 36	195 = 21
284 = 89	254 = 59	224 = 35	194 = 20
283 = 88	253 = 58	223 = 35	193 = 20
282 = 87	252 = 57	222 = 34	192 = 19
281 = 86	251 = 56	221 = 34	191 = 19
280 = 85	250 = 55	220 = 33	190 = 18
279 = 84	249 = 54	219 = 33	189 = 18
278 = 83	248 = 53	218 = 32	188 = 17
277 = 82	247 = 52	217 = 32	187 = 17
276 = 81	246 = 51	216 = 31	186 = 16
275 = 80	245 = 50	215 = 31	185 = 16
274 = 79	244 = 49	214 = 30	184 = 16
273 = 78	243 = 48	213 = 30	183 = 15
272 = 77	242 = 47	212 = 29	182 = 15
271 = 76	241 = 46	211 = 29	181 = 15
			180 = 15

really doesn't matter how you get into excellent physical shape; simply pick a program that works for you and keeps you from being injured. Many soldiers enjoy weight-lifting exercises that improve their ability to do push-ups. Some use aerobic machines or circuit programs to stay in top condition.

Whatever you decide to do, make it a part of your lifestyle that you intend to continue for the rest of your life. Physical fitness is a lifestyle decision. The ability to do very well on the Army physical fitness test will aid your career in whatever avenue you decide to pursue. Become familiar with the standards appropriate for your age and gender.

If you have a permanent profile in which a doctor has given you an alternate event for the run, then promotion points are based on how well you do on the other two events. By averaging the sit-up and push-up events, the overall score is reached. If you have a permanent profile for either the push-ups or the sit-ups, then that event will be scored as 60 out of 100.

Military Education Improvement

The Military Education section of the promotion system has been changed to reflect the Army's recent push for separation of the factors affecting promotion to E-5 and E-6. The points awarded have increased for both of these semicentralized promotions, but the ranks differ by several points.

For those soldiers competing for promotion to E-5, this area of the promotion packet is now worth 260 points, or 32.5 percent of the overall available score. For soldiers competing for promotion to E-6, this area of the promotion packet is now worth 280 points, representing 35 percent of the overall promotion packet potential.

There is also much more emphasis placed on the points awarded for the Warrior Leadership Course and the Advanced Leadership Course. Each of these courses is awarded a base value of 80 points with an additional 5 point values achievable for making the Commandant's List or for becoming a Distinguished Honor or Distinguished Leadership Graduate at each of these course levels. This means the soldier could be awarded up to 90 points total for each of these courses achieved at the appropriate grade level.

Success here is critical to your future success as a noncommissioned officer. Many of your educational improvement points will come from courses taken to fulfill Noncommissioned Officers Education System (NCOES) requirements. The NCOES network of training courses provides leadership, technical, and tactical training for every level of the NCO training cycle. Each of these courses parallels a particular grade and noncommissioned officer level of responsibility. Only soldiers holding the appropriate rank or currently on a corresponding promotion standing list are eligible for attendance. The NCOES network and other key programs of military education are described in more detail in Chapter 4.

Common rules governing the military education portion of your promotion packet are as follows:

- 80 points for WLC and ALC, regardless of rank and MOS, but any Army Correspondence Course Program (ACCP) requirements must be met before points are awarded.
- 4 points per week for each additional NCOES course (except ANCOC).
- Nonresident NCOES courses are calculated just like correspondence courses (1 for 5). Correspondence course credit is awarded based on 1 point for every five hours. Rounding is not allowed; only whole numbers are used (for example, eighteen hours are worth only 3 points).
- Ranger school is awarded 40 points, and the Special Forces qualification course is 60 points.
- 4 points per week for all other authorized military training.
- If you want credit, make sure you get a DA Form 87, Certificate of Training, signed by an LTC or higher. DA Form 87 is limited to recognized AR 350-1 training.
- ATTRS (Army Training Requirements and Reservation System) is the official record of training for all soldiers.
- Commanders and personnel officers are authorized to verify on-duty training (05 and above rule applies).

For most soldiers, success in the military education arena means correspondence courses. Not many soldiers can take enough military courses to fill this important area of the promotion packet. NCOES attendance is programmed to occur at different times in your military career. Most soldiers competing for promotion to SGT or SSG have had only one or two NCOES courses.

DEPARTMENT OF THE ARMY
CERTIFICATE OF TRAINING

THIS IS TO CERTIFY THAT

HAS SUCCESSFULLY COMPLETED

GIVEN AT _____   _____

DA FORM 87, 1 OCT 78

Certificate of Training

Soldiers frequently fail to complete correspondence course programs. The estimated completion rate for all the programs is less than 15 percent. Soldiers tend to complete only a few of the individual books. The reasons for lack of completion vary, but most probably stem from lack of self-discipline or personal accountability. Presumably, nothing happens to soldiers who enroll and fail to complete the required subcourses—nothing, that is, except lost promotion potential and unmet cutoff scores. One good technique for keeping current with your correspondence course completion goals is to date your books when you receive them. Then allow yourself one week to complete the books received.

There are many excellent ways to improve individual and unit success with correspondence courses. The unit commander or other leaders can set up group study courses and conduct training during the duty day. This can be done during low mission times, much like the "hip-pocket" training sessions of yesteryear. This works well if enforced. As long as it's done during the normal duty day, the commander can require soldier participation. It could also be used as a reward measure for top performance within the unit, as top performers could be given "study time" during the week especially designed to promote correspondence completion goals. Also, correspondence coursework can be tracked by the command and soldiers recognized and rewarded for excellent achievement. If your unit has no program like this, see your first sergeant or training NCO.

Civilian Education Improvement

The Civilian Education section of the promotion packet has received considerable reworking under the new semicentralized system; these changes are especially important to those competing for E-5. The Army decided to decrease the weight of civilian education for those competing for SGT-level promotions and retain the existing weight of this category for SSG or E-6 promotions. Foreign language proficiency is now emphasized more in this venue with the addition of a 10-point value for basic proficiency earned.

Civilian education is by far the weakest area in most soldiers' promotion packets. Soldiers receive 1 promotion point in the civilian education category for each semester hour completed. Moreover, the Army even provides *10 bonus points* as an incentive to soldiers to finish a degree program. These points can be earned as licensed certifications as well. This is the only area of the promotion packet in which a bonus exists. Soldiers can qualify for a one-time bonus after completing an associate's degree or higher while on active duty. If competing for E-6, the degree must have been completed after promotion to SGT.

So what prevents soldiers from taking college classes? A lack of time can be an important factor. Also, there may be a lack of interest in pursuing further education or apprehension at tackling college coursework. Whatever the reason, not having at least some college education has a long-term negative impact on a military career.

It is important to take enough college classes to get your military experience added on to a college transcript from an accredited institution. You do not need to determine whether the college is accredited or not; your local Education Center will take care of that for you. They will not award any tuition assistance for your class unless it meets the minimum accreditation standards. In order to get your military experience evaluated you need to take at least two 3-semester-hour classes. You need at least 6 semester hours of college class credit on your transcript in order for the military to accept your transcripted military experience for additional credit (see Chapter 6).

You should not be overly anxious about meeting this requirement. Even if you were a poor student in high school, you can probably find a college that will let you attend. The school might put you on academic probation to see how you do, but you will still get a transcript as long as you finish the classes satisfactorily. And there are many easy classes to take. You really can take basket-weaving if you want to.

There are probably some reading this who have absolutely no intention of taking a college class. Unfortunately, that is a common attitude among those who will eventually be forced out of the Army for failure to meet the retention control point objectives. It is never too late to have a change of heart. See if the following comparison between two promotion packets changes your mind about college. The only difference between the two is the presence or absence of civilian education.

E-5 Promotion Packet without College		E-5 Promotion Packet with College	
PT Test	130	PT Test	130
Awards	115	Awards	115
Military Education	210	Military Education	210
Civilian Education	0	Civilian Education	34
Marksmanship	85	Marksmanship	85
Deployment Experience	30	Deployment Experience	30
Total:	570	Total:	604

Note: The average promotion is 589 across all MOS Fields. Hence, this person would be promoted with additional education.

How does someone go from 0 to 34 points without taking a lot of college classes? It depends on the soldier's MOS and how long he or she was in military training. It also depends on how well that military training matches the training received by civilians in similar jobs.

Look at the breakdown of these 34 points as they may be evaluated by a college in your area:

Promotion Points	Source
3	Art Appreciation 101 class
3	Archery for Beginners 102 class
28	Military experience (see Chapter 6)
34	Points total

It is likely that the person with the civilian education points would get promoted ahead of the soldier without the credit, as 34 points is a significant difference. Take a close look at the next promotion point cutoff scores for the month. Observe how many times there were MOS promotions that fell between 570 and 604. On just about any given month, there will be anywhere from five to ten MOSs whose promotion point scores for E-5 fall between those two scores. It is difficult to argue that civilian education is not worth the two classes necessary to gain the benefits of civilian education points.

Promotion Board Performance

One of the big changes to the semicentralized promotion process is the elimination of promotion board points for those competing for promotion to E-5 and E-6. Promotion boards today are tailored to provide a Go/No Go verification of a unit commander's recommendation for promotion to this next level of service within the Army.

A typical promotion board is generally held at the battalion level. The members usually include the unit first sergeants, with the president of the board being the battalion command sergeant major. There is also a recorder present, generally from the Personnel Administration Center (PAC). These local boards are held for both E-5 and E-6 promotions.

The soldier reports to the president of the board and then is told to sit down for the questioning period. Each of the board members may ask the soldier questions on a specific subject. The board members will assess the soldier's uniform and appearance, military bearing, technical proficiency, and general military knowledge. Each of the board members rates the soldier's performance, and the scores are averaged to obtain the total. DA Form 3356 and DA Form 3357 show the Board Member Appraisal Worksheet and Board Recommendation scoring method. Studying these forms will help you prepare for your board appearance.

Many local boards are no longer using scoring methods, but rather Go/No Go for each of the areas; this is a decision that is made at the local board level.

BOARD MEMBER APPRAISAL WORKSHEET

For use of this form, see AR 600-8-19; the proponent agency is DCSPER.

1. NAME	2. RECOMMENDED GRADE	3. RECOMMENDED MOS

4. Board Interview and Evaluation and Points Awarded

AREAS OF EVALUATION	AVERAGE (1-7 Points)	ABOVE AVERAGE (8-13 Points)	EXCELLENT (14-19 Points)	OUTSTANDING (20-25 Points)	TOTAL POINTS
a. Personal Appearance, Bearing, and Self-Confidence					
b. Oral Expression and Conversational Skills					
c. Knowledge of World Affairs					
d. Awareness of Military Programs					
e. Knowledge of Basic Soldiering *(Soldier's Manual) (See note.)*					
f. Soldier's Attitude *(includes leadership and potential for promotion, trends in performance, etc).*					
g. TOTAL POINTS AWARDED					

NOTE: Questions concerning the knowledge of basic soldiering will be tailored to include land navigation, survival, night operations, inclement weather operations, adverse environment, and terrain.

5. REMARKS

6. ☐ I DO ☐ I DO NOT Recommend the Soldier for Promotion

7. SIGNATURE OF BOARD MEMBER	8. RANK	9. DATE *(YYYYMMDD)*

DA FORM 3356, MAY 2000   PREVIOUS EDITIONS ARE OBSOLETE   USAPA V1.00

Board Member Appraisal Worksheet

BOARD RECOMMENDATION

For use of this form, see AR 600-8-19; the proponent agency is DCS, G-1.

1. NAME	2. RECOMMENDED GRADE	3. RECOMMENDED MOS

4. BOARD MEMBER'S APPRAISAL WORKSHEET RESULTS

BOARD MEMBER'S NAME	RECOMMENDED		POINTS AWARDED (Transfer from DA Form 3356, Items 4a through 4g)						BOARD MEMBER TOTAL
	YES	NO	A	B	C	D	E	F	G
				5. COMBINED BOARD POINTS					
				6. DIVIDE TOTAL IN ITEM 6 BY THE NUMBER OF VOTING BOARD MEMBERS TO OBTAIN POINTS AWARDED					

7. Individual ☐ IS ☐ IS NOT Recommended for promotion by a majority of the board members.

8. REMARKS

9. TYPED OR PRINTED NAME AND SIGNATURE OF RECORDER	10. RANK	11. DATE (YYYYMMDD)

DA FORM 3357, MAY 2010   PREVIOUS EDITIONS ARE OBSOLETE.   APD PE v1.00ES

Board Recommendation

For promotion purposes, the Go/No Go decision is what is important for the promotion packet. Some local boards are using a Memorandum of Record to record their proceedings, with associated recommendations for Go/No Go.

There are a variety of ways in which to effectively prepare for the promotion board. Practice boards are often conducted at the unit level to aid soldiers. These are very beneficial, as practice is a vital element in doing well in a stressful situation. Soldier-of-the-month boards are another good way of practicing board skills, particularly if unit-level practice boards are unavailable.

Uniform and personal appearance must be outstanding. A good haircut, a dry-cleaned uniform, and highly polished shoes make the best impression. Consult AR 670-1 or your *Enlisted Soldier's Guide* for the proper wear of awards, badges, and insignia. Proper standing and correct sitting postures are important visible signs of respect to the board members. In addition, use a clear, respectful tone of voice when addressing the board members. Maintain eye contact, particularly with the board member who is asking the questions.

The most important aspect of addressing the board members is good knowledge of the material. You should become thoroughly versed in general military knowledge so that your answers are concise, responsive, and complete. There are several good study guides available, such as the *Soldier's Study Guide*, that can be used to properly prepare you for the board.

PROMOTION POINT REEVALUATIONS

The Army has migrated to a fully automated process for collecting score data from soldier files and local Military Personnel Offices. Under this new system, e-MILPO calculates scores in real time based on personnel and training data stored in the differing automated storage portals. These are captured at set times monthly to ensure fairness in the system and prevent duplication of effort and mistakes at various levels of command. This is meant to eliminate administrative requirements such as recomputations, reevaluations, and periodic verifications of scores. There is also no longer a minimum score for promotion required. The only minimum requirement for promotion is the APFT Score.

3

Senior Noncommissioned Officer Promotions, E-7 through E-9

THE HIGHEST LEVEL OF NCO RESPONSIBILITY

Senior noncommissioned officers serve in arguably the most important positions within the Army force structure. Proper selection into these demanding roles is so vital that the Army convenes a centralized board to ensure that only the most qualified are promoted. Senior noncommissioned officer promotions are very competitive, and the standards for promotions increase significantly with each higher grade. Individual job performance is the most important determining factor in these promotions. The level of difficulty of each job is also a major deciding factor in differentiating the degree of outstanding performance among noncommissioned officers.

Every noncommissioned officer is expected to set and enforce standards, provide professional leadership, and train his or her soldiers well. Senior NCOs need an even stronger educational base and professional array of skills in order to fulfill this role. They must demonstrate tactical and technical proficiency in their duties and have excellent ratings on their evaluation reports. The centralized Department of the Army (HQDA) promotion board will judge each candidate for promotion as indicated by the individual official military personnel file (OMPF).

PRIMARY AND SECONDARY ZONES OF CONSIDERATION

Criteria for primary and secondary zones of consideration for senior noncommissioned officer are announced for each board by the Department of the Army. The minimum time-in-service requirements are six, eight, and ten years for promotion to E-7, E-8, and E-9, respectively. Secondary zone considerations are much more competitive.

Each board determines the promotion selection criteria that ensure impartial consideration for the highest qualified noncommissioned officers in each

MOS. Specific reasons for selection or nonselection will not be provided to any person outside of the board. Board members are required by oath to comply with the established rules.

TYPICAL ORGANIZATION OF A CENTRALIZED BOARD

The HQDA deputy chief of staff for personnel (DCSPER) selects each board member. The members are commissioned officers and senior noncommissioned officers. The number of board members is determined by the number of records to be reviewed. Each board is broken into smaller groups or panels and will receive a letter of instruction (LOI) that outlines each of the individual board requirements.

The LOI establishes the required reports, the maximum number of NCOs to be selected, and any other administrative guidance necessary. No minimum selection criteria are given. Each promotion originates from a pool of fully qualified noncommissioned officers. Competition exists because the number of fully qualified NCOs is usually greater than the number of authorized positions available.

PREPARATION: THE KEY TO SUCCESS

The board will rate the quality of your performance and determine your promotion potential based on a physical review of your entire military file. The job performance impression you give is determined by the quality of your photograph, electronic record, and Personnel Qualification Record (PQR). How closely the board's impression matches reality depends on the quality of each of these items within the overall official military personnel file. You are the critical link in the quality of this review.

Your photograph will probably form the initial impression you make on each board member. "First impressions are lasting impressions," as the saying commonly goes. Make sure the board views you in a favorable light. Your uniform should be sharp and fit properly. Awards and decorations must be accurate and current. The photograph itself must be of top quality and present a clear and distinct professional image. Update your photograph regularly so that board members do not imagine that you have purposely delayed an update to hide a weight increase or similar problem. Likewise, a missing photograph conveys a problem or a lack of interest.

Your microfiche represents the majority of all your personnel files. It contains copies of awards and decorations, evaluation reports, Article 15s, enlistment documents, letters of commendation or recommendation, and various other administrative data. The information is arranged from oldest to newest and is read from left to right. The information needs to be checked for accuracy. Files often have incorrect or missing data and often even other soldiers' file information. An incorrect or poorly presented personal electronic file demonstrates a lack of attention to detail or an uncaring attitude. Keep yours current and request a new version any time there is a change to your military file.

Your Personnel Qualification Record consists of DA Form 2-1 and your Enlisted Record Brief (ERB). These two forms contain a brief history of your military career. They present duty assignment information, a physical fitness profile, soldier certifications, primary and secondary military occupational specialty data, authorized awards, badges, tabs, and skill identifiers. Soldiers often have conflicting information on these two forms, which confuses board members. The PQR is supposed to be certified by the soldier each time it is reviewed. A certified signature on an incorrect form raises doubt about the quality of the noncommissioned officer. Records can now be viewed and corrected using individual Army Knowledge Online (AKO) accounts. These AKO accounts help soldiers stay competitive with each career change.

CENTRALIZED BOARD PROCEEDINGS

Panel members vote on files based on a 1 to 6 scoring system. A 1 rating represents substandard performance; a 6 rating represents outstanding performance. Board members can also use + or – ratings to further weight a particular file. Three panel members rate each file and give it an individual rating. Each voting member does not know what rating was given by the other two panel members. The individual ratings are added together to get an overall file weight from –3 to +18.

Major differences in voting among panel members on an individual record are discussed during board deliberations. Sometimes a board member will notice something about a packet that may not have been noticed by the other two board members. The panel may request additional information about an NCO's record before a revote. Records are sent to other panels when agreement cannot be reached among members of a particular panel. Records are also rotated periodically to ensure that voting patterns are not established among board members.

Secondary zone selections are made from records that are considered outstanding in every area. The fully qualified noncommissioned officers from both zones are given an order of merit ranking based on their numerical score. The packets that have obtained the highest scores are considered the best-qualified for promotion. The final board recommendation is sent to the US Total Army Personnel Command (PERSCOM) in alphabetical order to be assigned a promotion sequence number. PERSCOM determines the sequence numbers by date of rank (DOR), basic active service date (BASD), and age, in that order.

UNDERSTANDING BOARD RESULTS

Every board is different, but there are common trends among them. Here is a possible scenario of how a board determines the point structure for ranking NCOs.

Number	Possible Qualifiers for SFC Selection
6+	Sergeant Morales/Audie Murphy selection, 4+ years of college, 2+ years as platoon sergeant
6	Post/division NCO QTR, 3+ years of college, 1+ year as platoon sergeant
6-	2+ years of college, 6 months to 1 year as platoon sergeant, 300 PT test
5+	Drill sergeant/recruiting duty, NCO Academy, 1+ year of college
5	JRTC/NTC OC duty, BDE NCO QTR, 6 months to 1 year of college, master fitness
5-	3 to 5 college classes, 90 days as platoon sergeant, ANCOC graduate
4+	Section chief, BN NCO QTR, 1 to 2 college classes, 290+ PT
4	ANCOC selectee, BN/BDE NCO month, 270–289 PT
4-	1 college class, strong jobs
3+	AR 600-9 qualified
3	Passed PT
3-	BNCOC, HS/GED
2+	1 needs improvement on NCOER
2	1 overweight
2-	1 PT failure
1+	2 needs improvements on NCOER
1	2 overweights, 1 DWI/1 DUI
1-	2 PT failures

What exactly do all those numbers mean? All the files are assigned numbers from 1- to 6+, with 3s being fully qualified for promotion, 2s awaiting next year's relook, and 1s being sent off to "QMP land" and selective early-retirement boards. Normally all of the 5 and 6 packets are promoted. These include the typical secondary zone promotion packets. You will probably not be promoted from the secondary zone unless you are at least a number 5-, with the probability increasing dramatically as you move up the scale. The number 4 packets usually get promoted, and every once in a while a number 3 packet will be selected. Has anyone ever gotten promoted outside of these guidelines? Of course. But it was probably because the Army was critically short of senior noncommissioned officers in a particular career field. Usually there are more than enough qualified candidates to go around.

FACTORS IN SECONDARY ZONE PROMOTIONS

Secondary zone promotion time lines for senior NCOs are six, eight, and ten years. There are very few sergeants major with only ten years of active-duty service. Generally E-5s make staff sergeant at eight to ten years of service. Most will make E-7 four to six years later and hold that rank until retirement. A few will pin on master sergeant or first sergeant rank with about eighteen years of service.

There is a definite gap between the authorized earliest promotion period and the real pin-on time frame. This is an area in which most soldiers accept the status quo. Army promotions for senior-level noncommissioned officers are very competitive. However, there are plenty of things the individual NCO can do to increase his or her chances for promotion. Board results show that there are a few main factors that cause some soldiers to be promoted over others, including an increased focus on higher education, holding key positions, and understanding the promotion board selection process.

Education and Secondary Zone Selections

Civilian education is certainly a major factor in secondary zone promotions. Sergeant first class promotions make up the majority of all senior noncommissioned officer promotions. In recent years, there has been a shift toward more education among the senior NCO ranks. A large percentage of all the promotable SSGs from recent boards have had a year or more of college education. The percentage is dramatically higher if you look solely at the secondary zone selectees. The importance of education increases with each subsequent rank; just look at the statistics included with each selection list released.

Many NCOs have their military education evaluated when they are sergeants or staff sergeants. The credit allowed for military experience changes with each promotion. Take the time to have your college transcripts updated to reflect this additional military experience. (Review the information in Chapter 6 before doing so.)

Jobs with Promotion Potential

Regardless of the job title, it is mandatory to do very well to be competitive. The type of job you hold and the perceived difficulty of the job also have a definite impact on promotion potential. Promotion boards tend to award more favorable ratings for promotions among noncommissioned officers who excel in traditionally tough jobs.

Statistically, the strongest jobs for potential promotion to E-7 are in the drill sergeant or recruiting areas. Recent centralized promotion boards have also placed a high degree of weight on inspector general (IG) jobs, equal opportunity (EO) advisor roles, and active component/reserve component (AC/RC) training support positions. Moreover, a careful study of board selection patterns indicates *a much higher rate of promotions for those who hold these positions early in their staff sergeant careers.* This changes significantly after promotion, however. It is then better to return to troops and line units and the hard platoon sergeant jobs. Some E-7s may be fortunate enough to find a first sergeant position, which is better still. Staff jobs held in positions authorized for the next higher grade also tend to look good if you receive a good NCO Evaluation Report.

Another favorable job for a young E-7 is as an observer-controller at either the National Training Center (NTC) at Fort Irwin, California, or the Joint

Good E-6 and E-7 Jobs

- Drill Sergeant
- Recruiter
- Observer-Controller
- Platoon Sergeant
- First Sergeant
- NCO Academy Instructor
- EO Advisor
- IG Duties
- AC/RC Liaison

Readiness Training Center (JRTC) at Fort Polk, Louisiana. These are difficult jobs and are recognized as such by the selection boards. Observer-controller jobs are solid positions regardless of grade. NCO Academy jobs are also statistically strong career moves.

Noncommissioned Officer Evaluation Reports (NCOERs)

Although some jobs definitely carry more weight than others, no job will increase your promotion potential unless it is substantiated by a strong evaluation report. A weak job with a strong evaluation report is better than a tough job with an average or mediocre report. Undoubtedly, there are many NCOs who perform well but receive weak evaluations. Bullet comments on an NCOER *must demonstrate* excellent performance. Excellent performance should manifest itself in some manner. The key is to correctly capture the tangible ways in which an NCO performed that made him or her an outstanding leader. Flowery words do not help NCOs get promoted. Only clear, obvious examples of excellent behavior will count when scrutinized by selection boards.

Stated Excellence	**Demonstrated Excellence**
Outperforms everyone else in physical fitness.	Scored 295 on most recent APFT; placed third in local marathon; increased overall section PT scores by 20 percent.
Absolutely the best NCO in the company.	Won Environmental NCO of the Year award; selected twice for special escort duty; wrote article for post newspaper.
Unmatched technical and tactical competence.	Completed two correspondence courses; took two additional classes toward degree; awarded Expert Field Medical Badge.

Study and memorize Part IV of DA Form 2166-8, NCO Evaluation Report. These are the NCO values and responsibility areas on which your performance will be evaluated. You will want to receive a rating of excellent in each. This can be done by ensuring the listed attributes become part of your daily duty performance.

Good NCOERs are not created by accident. A properly prepared evaluation report takes time and must be thoroughly researched and documented. The NCOER is too important a promotion document for careless handling. You have a big role as a rated NCO. You should provide your rater and senior rater with good input. Document your activities throughout the rating period. Look at every area of your influence, and make sure you adequately address your contributions to the unit. Use DA Pamphlet 623-205 as a reference tool for guidance on how to adequately record standards of performance. The following example shows the difference between a flowery report that merely makes statements of excellence and a substantiated report that demonstrates excellence.

NCO of the Month, Quarter, or Year

Do not pass up a chance to go to NCO of the Month and Quarter boards. Many NCOs disregard them once they pin on staff sergeant. These boards still carry a lot of weight at a promotion board and even more weight at the division or post level, regardless of rank. The counterpart boards among the schools also boost promotion potential. Board members tend to rate Drill Sergeant of the Cycle, Instructor of the Year, and similar achievements as evidence of professional excellence.

Physical Fitness and Appearance

High scores on unit physical fitness tests count heavily in individual packet weight, and you don't necessarily have to have a 300 score. Even scores of 270 and better tend to show up in higher grade promotion results. Physical Fitness Badge winners and Master Fitness Training Course attendees have garnered an equally impressive level of respect from recent boards. Unusual physical fitness events also count heavily—participation in marathons, biathlons, and other types of competition definitely stands out to board members.

Physical appearance is also very important to promotions. Many soldiers in excellent physical condition exceed the normal height and weight standards and have to submit to body fat analysis on Army Weight Control Program guidelines. The problem will be alleviated if an NCO can substantiate great physical condition in some other manner, such as extremely high PT scores or a photo that resembles Rambo. If you do not look like Rambo and cannot max the PT test, then do something that either brings you within standard or offsets the negative image.

NCO EVALUATION REPORT
For use of this form, see AR 623-3; the proponent agency is DCS, G-1.

FOR OFFICIAL USE ONLY (FOUO)
SEE PRIVACY ACT STATEMENT
IN AR 623-3.

PART I - ADMINISTRATIVE DATA

a. NAME *(Last, First, Middle Initial)*

b. SSN

c. RANK ( )

d. DATE OF RANK

e. PMOSC

f.1. UNIT   ORG.   STATION   ZIP CODE OR APO,   MAJOR COMMAND

f.2. STATUS CODE

g. REASON FOR SUBMISSION

h. PERIOD COVERED		i. RATED MONTHS	j. NON-RATED CODES	k. NO. OF ENCL	l. RATED NCO'S EMAIL ADDRESS *(.gov or .mil)*	m. UIC	n. CMD CODE	o. PSB CODE
FROM	THRU							
YEAR MONTH DAY	YEAR MONTH DAY							

PART II - AUTHENTICATION

a. NAME OF RATER *(Last, First, Middle Initial)*   SSN   SIGNATURE   DATE *(YYYYMMDD)*

RANK   PMOSC/BRANCH   ORGANIZATION   DUTY ASSIGNMENT   RATER'S AKO EMAIL ADDRESS *(.gov. or .mil)*

b. NAME OF SENIOR RATER *(Last, First, Middle Initial)*   SSN   SIGNATURE   DATE *(YYYYMMDD)*

RANK   PMOSC/BRANCH   ORGANIZATION   DUTY ASSIGNMENT   SENIOR RATER S AKO EMAIL ADDRESS *(.gov. or .mil)*

c. NAME OF REVIEWER *(Last, First, Middle Initial)*   SSN   SIGNATURE   DATE *(YYYYMMDD)*

RANK   PMOSC/BRANCH   ORGANIZATION   DUTY ASSIGNMENT   REVIEWER'S AKO EMAIL ADDRESS *(.gov. or .mil)*

d. ☐ CONCUR WITH RATER AND SENIOR RATER EVALUATIONS   ☐ NONCONCUR WITH RATER AND/OR SENIOR RATER EVAL *(See attached comments)*

e. RATED NCO: I understand my signature does not constitute agreement or disagreement with the evaluations of the rater and senior rater. I further understand my signature verifies that the administrative data in Part I, the rating officials in Part II, the duty description to include the counseling dates in Part III, and the APFT and height/weight entries in Part IVc are correct. I have seen the completed report. I am aware of the appeals process of AR 623-3.

SIGNATURE   DATE *(YYYYMMDD)*

PART III - DUTY DESCRIPTION *(Rater)*

a. PRINCIPAL DUTY TITLE

b. DUTY MOSC

c. DAILY DUTIES AND SCOPE *(To include, as appropriate, people, equipment, facilities and dollars)*

d. AREAS OF SPECIAL EMPHASIS

e. APPOINTED DUTIES

f. COUNSELING DATES   INITIAL   LATER   LATER   LATER

PART IV - ARMY VALUES/ATTRIBUTES/SKILLS/ACTIONS *(Rater)*

a. ARMY VALUES. Check either "YES" or "NO". *(Bullet Comments are mandatory. Substantive bullet comments are required for "NO" entries.)*   YES   NO

		YES	NO
V **A** **L** **U** **E** **S** Loyalty Duty Respect Selfless-Service Honor Integrity Personal Courage	1. LOYALTY: Bears true faith and allegiance to the U. S. Constitution, the Army, the unit, and other Soldiers.		
	2. DUTY: Fulfills their obligations.		
	3. RESPECT/EO/EEO: Treats people as they should be treated.		
	4. SELFLESS-SERVICE: Puts the welfare of the nation, the Army, and subordinates before their own.		
	5. HONOR: Lives up to all the Army values.		
	6. INTEGRITY: Does what is right - legally and morally.		
	7. PERSONAL COURAGE: Faces fear, danger, or adversity *(physical and moral).*		
	Bullet comments		

DA FORM 2166-8, OCT 2011   PREVIOUS EDITIONS ARE OBSOLETE.   Page 1 of 2
APD PE v1.02ES

NCO Evaluation Report

RATED NCO'S NAME *(Last, First, Middle Initial)*		SSN	THRU DATE

PART IV *(Rater)* **- VALUES/NCO RESPONSIBILITIES**   *Bullet comments are mandatory. Substantive bullet comments are required for "EXCELLENCE" or "NEEDS IMPROVEMENT."*

b. COMPETENCE
- o Duty proficiency; MOS competency
- o Technical & tactical; knowledge, skills, and abilities
- o Sound judgment
- o Seeking self-improvement; always learning
- o Accomplishing tasks to the fullest capacity; committed to excellence

EXCELLENCE *(Exceeds std)*	**SUCCESS** *(Meets std)*	**NEEDS IMPROVEMENT** *(Some)* *(Much)*

c. PHYSICAL FITNESS & MILITARY BEARING

APFT   HEIGHT/WEIGHT   /

- o Mental and physical toughness
- o Endurance and stamina to go the distance
- o Displaying confidence and enthusiasm; looks like a Soldier

EXCELLENCE *(Exceeds std)*	**SUCCESS** *(Meets std)*	**NEEDS IMPROVEMENT** *(Some)* *(Much)*

d. LEADERSHIP
- o Mission first
- o Genuine concern for Soldiers
- o Instilling the spirit to achieve and win
- o Setting the example; Be, Know, Do

EXCELLENCE *(Exceeds std)*	**SUCCESS** *(Meets std)*	**NEEDS IMPROVEMENT** *(Some)* *(Much)*

e. TRAINING
- o Individual and team
- o Mission focused; performance oriented
- o Teaching Soldiers how; common tasks, duty-related skills
- o Sharing knowledge and experience to fight, survive and win

EXCELLENCE *(Exceeds std)*	**SUCCESS** *(Meets std)*	**NEEDS IMPROVEMENT** *(Some)* *(Much)*

f. RESPONSIBILITY & ACCOUNTABILITY
- o Care and maintenance of equipment/facilities
- o Soldier and equipment safety
- o Conservation of supplies and funds
- o Encouraging Soldiers to learn and grow
- o Responsible for good, bad, right & wrong

EXCELLENCE *(Exceeds std)*	**SUCCESS** *(Meets std)*	**NEEDS IMPROVEMENT** *(Some)* *(Much)*

PART V - OVERALL PERFORMANCE AND POTENTIAL

a. RATER. Overall potential for promotion and/or service in positions of greater responsibility.

AMONG THE BEST	FULLY CAPABLE	MARGINAL

b. RATER. List 3 positions in which the rated NCO could best serve the Army at his/her current or next higher grade.

_____

_____

_____

e. SENIOR RATER BULLET COMMENTS

c. SENIOR RATER. Overall performance

1	2	3	4	5
		Successful	Fair	Poor

d. SENIOR RATER. Overall potential for promotion and/or service in positions of greater responsibility.

1	2	3	4	5
		Superior	Fair	Poor

DA FORM 2166-8, OCT 2011

Page 2 of 2
APD PE v1.02ES

NCO Evaluation Report *continued*

Sergeant Morales and Audie Murphy Clubs

Make every effort to be selected as a member of a distinguished organization, such as the Sergeant Morales or Audie Murphy Club. Such a membership denotes excellence in several arenas, and promotion boards know that selection criteria are extremely high and normally only the best NCOs make the cut. Check for information on local chapter membership requirements.

NCOES Schools and Courses

Lately there seems to be an Army-wide trend for senior noncommissioned officers to delay their NCOES school attendance. The only good reason to do so belongs to an E-7 who has a chance to serve for ninety days or more as a first sergeant. It may prove more beneficial to take this position, which can be key to early selection for promotion. You certainly do not want to risk losing the slot to someone else or being considered for a secondary promotion to the next rank without having attained the next level in the NCOES ladder. Some of this may seem trite to seasoned NCOs, but the numbers show its importance. People are passing up opportunities to excel in this area every day.

Licensures and Certifications

Special licenses and certifications for skill sets earned through the civilian sector are now worth 10 points. Soldiers can add up to five separate licenses and/or certifications to their packets for a maximum of 50 potential points for this category. This policy reflects the military's growing awareness of the need to have a targeted education process for soldiers so that they are developing skill sets that positively impact their level of expertise and functionality within military occupational specialty fields. Military occupational specialties affected by these changes can be accessed at www.cool.army.mil.

PART II

The Role of Education

4

Military Education

A professional military education is an absolute imperative for leaders in today's Army. The military environment is constantly changing, and soldier skills must remain current in order to maintain a competent Army. Noncommissioned officers are responsible for the individual training of soldiers. This great responsibility requires that they receive excellent training in military skills and professional leadership. Leaders will only be able to pass on the degree of knowledge that has been imparted to them. There are several avenues available for noncommissioned officers and other future leaders to acquire the skills necessary to gain this level of competence.

THE NONCOMMISSIONED OFFICER EDUCATION SYSTEM (NCOES)

The most important leadership skills development available to noncommissioned officers is provided in the NCOES training courses. There are four levels: primary, basic, advanced, and senior.

The Primary Leadership Development Course (PLDC) is for specialists and corporals and is designed to teach them the professional leadership skills necessary to perform as a sergeant. PLDC is worth 16 points to soldiers competing for semicentralized promotions to the sergeant and staff sergeant ranks. The course was formerly non-MOS specific and built around basic soldier and leadership skills needed to lead soldiers at the squad level; it was four weeks long and taught at NCO academies worldwide. This course has since been replaced with the Warrior Leader Course (WLC), which is designed to build more independent leadership skills. Previous PLDC coursework will still be recognized for promotion to SGT and SSG. The Warrior Leader Course is worth 80 points.

The Basic Noncommissioned Officers Course (BNCOC) represents the next level of the NCOES. This course of instruction prepares sergeants for promotion to staff sergeant. There are two types of BNCOC courses: One for those from combat-related fields, and another for combat support and combat service support soldiers. Soldier leaders from direct combat-related fields receive combat-critical training in operating and employing their weapons in a combatlike environment. The emphasis is on teaching these sergeants how to train their crews, section, or squads in combat-critical tasks. These courses are taught at the NCO academies, and local commanders decide who will attend. The course of instruction differs significantly for combat support and combat service support soldiers. These junior leaders are taught MOS-related and common core tasks. These BNCOC courses build on the prior training received in PLDC and are taught at the resident service schools. The US Total Army Military Personnel Command (PERSCOM) manages the selection process, and local commanders have the option of approving, deferring, or substituting for the candidate. The length of the course depends on the MOS and can vary greatly. In all cases, the promotion value is 80 points.

The Advanced Noncommissioned Officers Course (ANCOC) represents the advanced level of training given to staff sergeants and sergeants first class to prepare them for platoon sergeant and similar duties. An HQDA selection board chooses NCOs annually to attend this very important advanced level of training. The competition for selection is intense, and the evaluation criteria are similar to that described under senior noncommissioned officer board selections. Many noncommissioned officers find that they are selected for promotion while awaiting a school slot for ANCOC. The classes are taught at the service schools, but much of the common core curriculum is developed by the US Army Sergeants Major Academy (USAMA). ANCOC attendance cannot be used for semicentralized promotion competition.

Military education training at the most senior level is accomplished through training at the Sergeants Major Course (SMC) taught at the US Army Sergeants Major Academy. Selection into the SMC is highly selective, and only the top contenders at the E-8 level may attend. Master sergeants and first sergeants in the published zone for selection must request consideration. The course of instruction is twenty-two weeks long, and only two resident classes are taught each year. Noncommissioned officers in the selection zone may also request an alternate seat at either the US Navy Senior Enlisted Academy or the US Air Force NCO Academy. There are also opportunities to take a corresponding studies program. The training material closely coincides with the material taught at the SMC and is open to sergeants first class (promotable) through sergeants major. The corresponding studies program is also competitive and based on a DA selection board.

NCOES FUNCTIONAL COURSES

The Operations and Intelligence Course trains senior noncommissioned officers in the duties expected of intelligence or operations sergeants at the battalion and higher levels of command. These staff functions are considered especially important and are not easily gained through experience alone. Each of the major commands receives annual allocations for this eight-week school. The only other functional course is the First Sergeants Course taught at the US

Army Sergeants Major Academy. This eight-week course trains sergeants first class and master sergeants in the critical skills necessary to properly run a unit. The curriculum stresses the correct procedures for unit administration, logistics, physical fitness training, discipline, and problem solving. Consult AR 614-200 for the required procedures and forms for requesting specific training programs and related duty assignments.

ARMY CORRESPONDENCE COURSE PROGRAM (ACCP)

The Army Correspondence Course Program (ACCP) is an excellent avenue for professional development that greatly benefits soldiers of every rank. Correspondence courses represent portable training that probably would not be available to most soldiers through a resident training course. Resident training is expensive and cannot be liberally applied throughout the force structure. Correspondence courses fill a big gap in building a professional Army. These courses are built on the premise of self-study and can be used to develop specific skills needed by individual leaders in a variety of circumstances. The courses are developed by the proponent schools for each subject matter. For instance, a course in infantry tactics is developed through the Infantry Center and School.

Correspondence courses can be ordered on just about any subject imaginable, with very few restrictions; however, some courses may require special clearances, or they may limit enrollment to certain military occupational specialty classifications. But even courses that do have limitations can often be taken with a waiver authorization from the unit commander. Subject matter can be pursued through either an entire course of study or selected individual books, which are called subcourses. There are several avenues through which one can obtain books or courses. Correspondence course study can even be completed through material provided by other military services. The Army Correspondence Course Program Catalog, DA Pamphlet 351-20, is now available as an electronic publication through epubs@usapa.army.mil (as are many other publications and forms) or as part of the Army Electronic Library on CD. These CDs are available by mail through the US Army Publishing Agency and its distribution operations facility at 1655 Woodson Road, St. Louis, MO 63114-6128.

Many soldiers have discovered the value of correspondence courses in gaining promotion points. This is definitely a rewarding path, even though the Army has now changed the program to allow credit only for completed courses (not individual books). The amount of credit depends on the total awarded credit for the entire course.

Soldiers earn 1 promotion point for every 5 correspondence book hours. Some books are worth more than others. Total hours can also be added together to gain more promotion points. Correspondence courses are still valuable tools even without their promotion point value, as professional skills are always worth developing. Each course completed can be added to your official military personnel file. This additional self-taught training makes you more competitive for promotion at every level of the Army's promotion system. And the skills developed through individual study will enhance your ability to lead soldiers. Many of these courses now count toward civilian education credit as well. Course completion certificates can be turned into civilian transcript credit. The American Council on Education's *Guide to the Evaluation of Educational Experiences in the Armed Services* gives the recommended equivalent college credit for many of these correspondence courses.

Additional correspondence course material that can be used for training and promotion credit is available through the following online repositories:

• Federal Emergency Management (FEMA) courses—www.training.fema.gov
• Marine Corps correspondence courses—www.mci.usmc.mil
• Medical correspondence courses—www.atrrs.army.mil/selfdevctr
• Reimer Digital Library (TRADOC)—www.adtdl.army.mil
• Army correspondence course enrollment—www.atsc.army.mil/accp

MOS CLASSIFICATION AND RECLASSIFICATION

The military occupational specialty (MOS) that you hold definitely affects the avenues available for career development and career progression. Overages and shortages can affect every MOS at one time or another. The Army tries to manage occupational specialties so that they remain balanced throughout a soldier's career, but delicate balance is difficult to manage in an ever-changing army. Weapon systems and technologies can become outdated, and priorities and missions change. Evaluate your career field regularly and make the necessary changes to stay current with the needs of the Army. Exercise sensible judgment and move out of career fields that are severely overstrength or becoming obsolete. Normally, promotion rates slow down considerably in overstrength or obsolete military occupational specialties.

Moving from an overstrength MOS to an understrength MOS is usually fairly easy to do. Often all it requires is a formal request through your Personnel Service Center. The process is made easier because it involves meeting a known need of the Army. Usually a transfer of military occupational specialties involves a permanent-change-of-station (PCS) move. Frequently you will be sent to another service school en route to your next duty station. A change of MOS may also open up opportunities for additional training. Having soldiers attend schools en route to their final destination often saves the Army considerable money. The chances for additional training are significantly improved if requested early enough to match class availability slots with PCS movement orders.

Soldiers who are already on a promotion standing list for either sergeant or staff sergeant may get promoted almost immediately to the next higher grade. This happens with most voluntary reclassifications and some mandatory reclassifications, because the soldier begins to compete for promotion on the first day of the month following official reclassification. Many soldiers who did not have enough points for promotion in an overstrength MOS find that point requirements are much lower for the new MOS.

Mandatory reclassifications, where the Army dictates a reclassification, often come with a special identifier (4A) that postpones promotion until service school requirements are met for the new MOS. In this case, a soldier may meet a monthly cutoff score but not be promoted until after he or she graduates from the service school for the new MOS. Here the eligible date of promotion and the effective date of promotion will be different. Back pay will not be authorized, because pay and allowances are based on effective dates of promotion.

Procedures for requesting an MOS change are outlined in AR 135-205. The administrative prerequisites for each MOS can be found in AR 611-201. Some MOS changes can actually earn you money; check with your local reenlistment NCO to see if there are shortage MOSs that have bonus incentives. Make a thorough assessment of the career progression and career development paths of any projected MOS before committing to a possible irreversible decision. Although MOS reclassifications are often smart career moves, the school training received does not have any promotion point value. The 4-point-per-week rule does not apply to MOS-producing schools.

Special Note: The Army has changed the delivery methodology and location of the majority of the current regulations, DA Pamphlets, forms, and similar publications. Many of these publications are now available only through electronic media at armypubs.army.mil. In some cases, the conversion includes merging of existing publications and renaming of reference titles. This website cross-references new and preexisting nomenclatures when necessary.

SOLDIER TRAINING COURSES

Soldier training courses are courses of instruction that are established by unit installation commanders to sustain technical skills required of certain soldiers. Sometimes the courses are resourced through the Education Service Office. These courses are generally easier to get into than traditional Army service school courses. They are worth promotion points if they are of at least one week's duration. (A week can be either an actual calendar five-day work week or forty classroom hours.) These courses are worth 4 promotion points per week. The following list represents typical soldier training courses that would be conducted on most major installations and which fall under the 4-points-per-week rule:

- Nuclear, Biological, and Chemical (NBC) defense.
- Unit supply clerk.
- Forklift operator.
- The Army Maintenance Management System (TAMMS).
- Prescribed load list (PLL) clerk.

- Unit postal clerk.
- Word processing and data management.
- Unit Level Logistics System (ULLS).
- Ammunition handler.
- Unit armorer.
- Unit supply operations and management.
- Fuel handler.
- Bus driver.
- Safety officer.
- Hazardous waste (HW) management.
- Motor pool operations and management.

MAJOR ARMY COMMAND (MACOM)-SPONSORED TRAINING COURSES

MACOM training courses may be easily available to some soldiers provided they are stationed in an area that supports these centers. Many of the NCOES schools are MACOM-sponsored. Major commands provide training, materials, staff, and validation for many of the special skill-development training courses, such as the Jungle Operations Training Center, Northern Warfare Training Center, certain Air Assault Schools, and many of the local foreign language training centers. These courses are worth 4 points per week of training.

MASTER FITNESS TRAINING

Master fitness trainers are soldiers who have completed one of the approved Master Fitness Training Courses. They are an invaluable asset to unit commanders because they are trained in the scientific elements of physical fitness. The Army Physical Fitness School at Fort Jackson, South Carolina, trains physical fitness leaders. Normally only the best noncommissioned officers are allowed to attend this school, worth 4 points per week of training.

The Master Fitness Training School has also rolled out a training program that conducts on-site training of Master Fitness leaders at major Army installations. The two-part course is divided between Army correspondence training and actual hands-on/classroom training conducted locally. The Master Fitness School will also continue to be available for course completion through the Fort Jackson training program.

COMBAT LIFESAVER COURSE

Combat lifesavers are nonmedical soldiers who have been trained to conduct lifesaving measures on casualties. The training is given in group-study fashion, using correspondence course training materials. A staff surgeon is designated to implement a successful program at brigade level and higher. Each unit is supposed to have a trained combat lifesaver for each crew, squad, or equivalent-size unit. Combat lifesavers must be recertified each year. This medical training is very useful for any soldier regardless of military occupational specialty and is worth 4 points per week of training.

OTHER SOURCES OF MILITARY EDUCATION AND TRAINING

Every installation has unique resources, classes, and training available to service the community of professional soldiers, and you should thoroughly research the possibilities in your area. Military education and any other type of training should be a continuous pursuit throughout your professional career. Learn to update skills regularly. The practice will enrich your military experience and pay big dividends in personal and professional growth. The following list represents some additional avenues that may be available for increasing your professional skills:

- Courses of training from other military services (except MOS-producing courses).
- Joint Airborne/Air Transportability Training or Airload Planners course.
- Amphibious training.
- Army Learning Centers (good resource centers for soldiers).
- Unit movement noncommissioned officer training.
- Army Apprenticeship Program (certain selected MOSs; see DA Pamphlet 621-200).
- Cyber-Based Instructional System on noncollegiate-sponsored instruction (see education counselor; available where CYBIS terminal is located).

OTHER RELATED REQUIREMENTS FOR MILITARY EDUCATION CREDIT

Training must be annotated and taken in accordance with military guidelines in order to be used for promotion point objectives. One of the primary guidelines is that the training must be completed during the normal duty day. This means that training conducted while on temporary-duty status or while on military leave would not be eligible for earning Military Education promotion points. Additionally, training received should be annotated on a DA Form 87, Certificate of Training, and conducted at battalion or higher level of command. Training conducted at the small-unit level (i.e. company, detachment, or similar level) is not eligible for certification and award of credit.

5

Civilian Education

YOU *CAN* GO TO COLLEGE

Going to college is an important part of any professional soldier's career-development plan. Civilian education is not only a component of the point system for sergeant promotions (75 points for E-5 and 100 points for E-6), it is also a great determiner of how both junior and senior enlisted soldiers are judged against their peers. And so far as personal development is concerned, there is nothing more highly recommended for obtaining knowledge beyond high school than the pursuit of higher education at the college level.

Though it would be difficult to argue the value to a soldier's career of taking even two classes, it is easy to find many soldiers willing to sidestep this important asset. A simple reason for this is that most soldiers are unfamiliar with the college process. College is often mistakenly thought unattainable for those who did not graduate at the top of their high school classes. Therefore, it is understandable that some soldiers may approach the possibility of attending college with uncertainty. Fortunately, the uncertainties about college disappear quickly once a soldier attends that first course. And, more fortunately, many soldiers find it such an enriching experience that they go on to achieve far more in their college experience than they originally thought possible. In addition, many soldiers find that their military training courses are more challenging than the typical beginning college course. With the exceptional training that soldiers receive today, most are equipped to handle the rigors of a typical college curriculum.

The purpose of this chapter is to make the "traditional" college experience both attainable and profitable to your career. Tips for entering college, saving time and money, and choosing the best program for your individual goals are discussed. As with your Army career, you are the ultimate determiner of how well you function within the educational arena, not only as to how well you do grade-wise, but also how you apply the college process to your unique situation of being a student who is also a soldier.

SERVICEMEMBERS OPPORTUNITY COLLEGES ARMY DEGREES (SOCAD)

Servicemembers Opportunity Colleges Army Degrees (SOCAD) is an Army-wide network of colleges offering a variety of technical or general areas of study. Frequently located on or near military installations, SOCAD institutions offer associate's and bachelor's degrees, as well as certificate programs. This Department of Defense contractual agreement gives soldiers the ability to complete programs with their original SOCAD-approved institution. Soldiers desiring the many benefits associated with this arrangement must obtain a SOCAD Student Agreement from a SOCAD-approved college.

The benefits of attending a SOCAD-approved college include limited residency requirements (no more than 25 percent of the degree program is required in residence at the institution); service school credit for military training that is based on the recommendations found in the American Council on Education (ACE) guide and that is appropriate to the curriculum; acceptance of nationally recognized standardized tests such as DANTES and CLEP (see Chapter 6); and transfer of comparable courses between colleges within the SOCAD network without prior approval from the original institution. This ability to transfer credit between member colleges is important because it lessens the impact of the many moves inherent in a military career. Refer to AR 621-5 for more information on the SOCAD network.

DEGREE PROGRAMS

Colleges and universities have a variety of degree programs, which are outlined in their catalogs. Typically, there are two-year associate's degrees, four-year bachelor's degrees, and more advanced degree programs at the master's and doctoral levels. The degree requirements are set by the institutions themselves and can be somewhat flexible to meet varying circumstances, such as those presented by soldiers. Schools that have programs offering the most flexibility to soldiers are those that take an active interest in the military community, such as schools with satellite campuses on the military installation (such as SOCAD institutions) and, typically, community colleges.

Although the more traditional two- and four-year colleges and universities in your area may be willing to work with you, they typically are most adept at serving their full-time students. More perseverance may be necessary to obtain assistance from these types of institutions, but if your career goals include an advanced degree from a prominent university, you will find helpful tips in the following information as well.

Associate's Degree Programs

The typical two-year associate in arts degree program requires the following:
- 60 semester hours of credit.
- 48 credits minimum in the general education area (made up of humanities, English classes, and arts and sciences electives).
- 12 elective hours.

The associate's degree-level courses are generally considered the first two years of college (at the 100 and 200 levels or freshman and sophomore levels in a four-year program). Community colleges are best known for offering a wide variety of two-year associate's degree programs. Such programs are often the best method for soldiers to break into college without making a complete four-year commitment. Also, the community colleges generally have less stringent entrance requirements and offer a variety of remedial courses for those who need them. Remedial classes are designed to provide high school equivalent preparation for basic knowledge in English, math, history, or the sciences. These classes can often be avoided by taking advantage of free tutorial services offered by many colleges and universities.

Bachelor's Degree Programs
The typical four-year Bachelor of Arts in liberal arts degree requires the following:
- At least 120 semester hours of college equivalent coursework.
- A minimum of 39 semester hours of upper-division (300 and 400 level) credit.
- A residency requirement (college classes actually taken at the institution).
- A lower-division basic liberal arts and general skills component.
- A declared major in a particular field of study.
- A demonstrated grasp of the subject matter (normally proven by grade point average).

Most colleges and universities have course-numbering systems that are used to differentiate lower-division (100 and 200 level) and upper-division (300 and 400 level) classes. Lower-division courses are taught at the freshman and sophomore levels. Junior and senior classes make up the upper-division baccalaureate structure and usually are taken after the lower-division requirements have been met. A little-known fact is that lower-division and upper-division requirements can be met simultaneously by carefully choosing classes that fulfill several degree constraints. (This is demonstrated in Chapter 10.)

Choosing a degree program can be difficult, particularly if you aren't sure of your exact interests. Most colleges offer free aptitude exams designed to help you discover career paths suited for you. These exams can be excellent tools that can ultimately save money and time by pinpointing your areas of interest and skill.

ADMISSION TO COLLEGE
The Education Center is an excellent source of help for soldiers wishing to attend college. The process of being admitted to college is made easier by seeking out the assistance of an education service officer or an education counselor. They have the ability to streamline the process, as they deal with the local colleges and with soldiers' unique needs on a daily basis. They will provide invaluable assistance in determining a degree path and choosing appropriate-level classes to meet the requirements of each program. They can also assist in

the entire paperwork process, including any required entrance examinations. Education counselors are usually very familiar with the local SOCAD network of colleges and will provide advice and assistance in getting your military experience documented accurately onto a civilian transcript. They also refer soldiers to the installation's testing control officers for taking standardized tests such as CLEP and DANTES.

PAYING FOR COLLEGE

The Army provides enough assistance with college costs that every soldier should be able to further his or her civilian education. Tuition assistance is available to help pay for college attendance for most active-duty soldiers—it currently pays for 100 percent of the tuition costs but does not cover books and other related expenses. Tuition assistance is a benefit available through morale and support funds provided at the Department of the Army level. This is an important benefit because it does not affect a soldier's individual educational funds earned as a result of active-duty service.

Education counselors can provide you with financial aid application forms when you register for a class. Tuition assistance can be used to pay for up to 15 semester hours of college (about five classes) per year. Some installations base the funding on $4,500 annually. The education counselor can also help with other forms of financial aid, such as Pell Grants and student loans. Additionally, you will probably need to visit the financial aid office of your college.

There are plenty of innovative methods of cutting college costs. Book costs, for example, can be very high. Buying used books rather than new ones can cut costs considerably. Additionally, local libraries often carry the textbooks, which you can borrow rather than buy. The professor of the course may even have an additional copy that can be borrowed. Soldiers taking the same course together can divide the cost by sharing the textbooks.

Approaching your unit commander with the idea of setting up a unit scholarship fund is another method of lowering tuition and book costs associated with college attendance. The college financial aid office can do all the paperwork to set up such a fund to benefit soldiers. Local businesses such as the post bank and credit union are good sources for scholarship donations. Scholarship donations are tax-deductible, and many organizations support similar projects all the time. The unit commander can decide who gets scholarship assistance.

There are many organizations within the military environment that offer scholarships to soldiers and their family members. Many soldiers, especially in the lower enlisted grades, have difficulty paying for books and other expenses not provided by the Army's tuition assistance. These alternative scholarship and financial sources can often mean the difference between attending college and not attending. See the sample letter for soldiers competing for these limited scholarship funds.

(Letterhead)

(Office Symbol)   (Date)

MEMORANDUM FOR: AUSA, Any Local Branch

SUBJECT: Letter of Recommendation for SPC John A. Doe

1. I believe SPC Doe would be an excellent choice for the AUSA Academic Grant Award. He is an extremely dedicated soldier who is constantly improving himself both during the duty day and after duty hours. SPC Doe was recently selected to be the Soldier of the Quarter for the Battalion. He is also scheduled to go before the February E-5 Promotion Board (well ahead of his peers).

2. SPC Doe is very motivated and quick to volunteer his efforts in many ways. He is usually seen carrying the unit guidon during battery runs and often assists with baby-sitting and/or Combat Lifesaver duties at unit parties or gatherings. He also volunteers his time to teach a 5th and 6th grade Sunday school class at a local church. He recently had an article published in the local paper.

3. SPC Doe is currently enrolled in two college classes and has taken five classes previously while assigned to XYZ Battery. I cannot imagine a more fully deserving or qualified applicant for the AUSA Scholarship Award. Please feel free to call or write to me for any additional information. My office telephone number is 123-4567.

                                        Commander's Name
                                        CPT, Branch
                                        Commanding

Sample Recommendation for College Grant Award

GOING TO CLASS

Doing well in college requires more than just showing up. Your strategy for excelling should begin prior to class registration. With the unique work style of the military, including a variety of deployments, it is advisable that students choose classes and professors wisely. If possible, contact potential professors before the class begins to determine whether they will be sympathetic toward your job requirements, which may include missing some classes during deployments.

A professor may be willing to issue you a class syllabus early. The syllabus includes an outline of the course curriculum, a list of textbooks required, the grading standards, and other course requirements, such as tests, papers, and presentations. The ability to obtain the course textbook and syllabus early can give you the flexibility to complete assignments before their normal due date, especially when you're anticipating deployment or other military duties during the semester. Many professors recognize the unique problems associated with military attendance and are more than willing to make the necessary arrangements with soldiers. Early and frequent communication is vitally important to this process.

TIPS FOR DEVELOPING A FLEXIBLE DEGREE PROGRAM

The following degree outline typifies the process needed to obtain a Bachelor of Arts degree in liberal arts with a major in management. This model will be used to demonstrate techniques that can be used to streamline your degree-seeking goals.

It is possible to combine degree requirements so that overall requirements are minimized. Philosophy, religion, political science, and literature classes are good targets for minimization goals, because many of these types of courses do not have prerequisite requirements for upper-level classes. (Prerequisite courses are those that must be completed in order to qualify for some higher-level courses. For example, one must successfully complete Math 101 before taking Math 201.) Many students automatically choose lower-division, introductory courses in these categories without examining the college catalog for upper-division course requirements. Students sometimes make the assumption that the upper-division courses are more work or beyond their capabilities. This is not necessarily the case, as some fields have courses whose subject matter can stand alone, with little relation to other courses.

For example, assume that this college offers several choices for the religion requirement in the basic skills/liberal arts component: Introduction to the New Testament (REL 101), Paul's Missionary Journeys (REL 301), New Age Theory (REL 454), and Introduction to Islam (REL 201). If you choose REL 101 and REL 201, you will satisfy the degree requirements satisfactorily, but if you choose REL 301 and REL 454, you satisfy two degree needs. These two courses meet the religion course requirements for 6 semester hours and also help satisfy the minimum upper-division 39-semester-hour constraint.

MODEL CURRICULUM

Basic Skills/Liberal Arts Component	Semester Hours	Management Component	Semester Hours
English Composition I	3	Principles of Accounting I	3
English Composition II	3	Principles of Accounting II	3
Mathematics	3	Managerial Accounting	3
Natural Science	6	Principles of Macroeconomics	3
Social Science	3	Principles of Microeconomics	3
Behavior Science	3	Principles of Finance	3
History/Political Science	6	Quantitative Methods	3
Humanities	6	Business Statistics	3
Religion	6	Business Law	3
Literature/Language/Speech	3	Principles of Management	3
Philosophy	6	Personnel Management	3
Free electives (classes you choose)	12	Managerial Communications	3
Total:	60	Managerial Policies and Strategies	3
		Organizational Behavior	3
		Free electives (classes you choose)	18
		Total:	60

A careful selection of classes that meet both these constraints could easily satisfy many of the total upper-division requisites. Every restraint lifted allows for more freedom in the overall degree program. This less-restrictive program then becomes moldable to your specific background, including military experience.

A great deal of the 120-hour minimum degree constraint can be satisfied through alternate sources. Soldiers often have more military experience and other untapped equivalent college credit than most degree programs can assimilate. Many military training courses are accepted for college credit. The trick is to be as smart as possible in matching military experience with college requirements and electives. The process of meeting two degree constraints with one class, as demonstrated above, is one effective method of lessening the required class load. By doing this, the soldier can plug in tangible experience, military classes, and equivalent college examinations where applicable. (College equivalency examinations and other forms of nontraditional credit are addressed in Chapter 6.)

Most colleges and universities have internal rules that they apply to ensure that their graduating students receive a quality, well-rounded education. Unless they are affiliated with the SOCAD program, many colleges tend to limit transfer credit so that entering students take the majority of required classes at their institution. They are literally in the business of selling education to the student body, so be sure to compare the credit-granting systems of the SOCAD colleges against those at the non-SOCAD institutions.

You must become familiar with these in-house boundaries and exercise assertive effort to ensure that your individual credit is fully counted. This is important, because the rules are rarely based on accreditation standards but are at the discretion of the individual school. Military experience and other forms of equivalent credit are recognized by the accreditation bodies as sufficient stand-alone credit. Convincing the colleges of the validity of your experience as compared with their coursework may be more difficult.

The model curriculum has a residency requirement of 30 semester hours toward its Bachelor of Arts degree. This means that you'll have to take at least a year's worth of classes at this institution in order to meet its guidelines. Most classes are based on a 3-semester-hour standard, which means you'll have to take at least ten classes with this college.

The college also limits equivalent test credit to a maximum of 30 semester hours of transfer credit. Most students would like to take and pay for only those classes absolutely necessary to meet requirements. The college, on the other hand, benefits from each class taken and thus is not as concerned about students possibly not choosing classes as efficiently as possible. Use intelligent forethought in the class-selection process so that you meet accreditation standards without sacrificing time and spending money needlessly.

WORKING SMARTER, NOT HARDER, IN COLLEGE

Most college classes have written assignments that must be done to meet syllabus objectives. Imagine yourself sitting in your first night of class for Religion 301 (Paul's Missionary Journeys). The first night of class, the professor hands out his syllabus and explains the course requirements. In this class, you will have to turn in two reports detailing the Apostle Paul's two missionary journeys. Each report will be at least five pages in length, typed and double-spaced, mechanically and grammatically correct, and properly referenced, with title and contents pages. The two reports each will be worth 25 percent of the course grade. There will be a midterm and final exam each also worth 25 percent of the total grade. Class attendance is expected, but reasonable allowances will be made for missed classes. Test nights are required attendance and will be excused only for medical illness or injury, other emergencies, or with prior professor approval.

This is what can be commonly expected of a college class. Some may require more work and some less, but all requirements are generally well outlined during the first class and in the course syllabus. How much time does it realistically take to complete the requirements for a college class? In this case, the two reports could probably both be done in one Saturday if you visit the library early and do your research well. Most good libraries have research assistants who have degrees in library research. These professionals can provide a wealth of assistance in finding the best resource material to complete your work and can help you with access to digital and other related resources.

If you are able to obtain the syllabus early, it might benefit you to begin research papers even before the first class. This is especially helpful when taking more than one class or when taking difficult or time-consuming subjects. The exams will probably be well explained by the professor, and you will know in advance what to expect in most cases. Very few professors surprise their students with exam content.

Another suggestion for optimum college success is to use some of your leave during peak study times. Try to take only Monday through Friday leave so that you have weekends on both ends of your study periods. This will allow you to maximize the number of weeks that you can take off from work. Thirty days of annual leave stretches pretty far when used in five-day increments.

FACING PROBLEMS IN COLLEGE

If you get into a course that is too difficult, you may want to withdraw before you are penalized with a failing grade. Every college has class-withdrawal guidelines. Become familiar with them beforehand and know how to use them wisely. A class that seems impossible under one professor may be a breeze under another.

If you miss the withdrawal deadline, talk with the professor frequently and get individual help from him or her and from other qualified students or tutors. Many colleges have tutors available free of charge. Also, do not be afraid to ask for additional assignments in order to make up for poor grades. Professors are often impressed by a student's determination to do well in a class despite individual weakness in a particular field.

GoArmyEd

The Army has created a new educational initiative aimed at getting enlisted soldiers more opportunities to complete a college degree and/or a certification program from virtually any location around the world. GoArmyEd is a virtual gateway to request tuition assistance, distance-learning classes, and college courses through an online network. The portal can be reached through Google and similar web portals and through any participating college or the eArmyU system. The system is interactive and very user-friendly for soldiers.

While this chapter dealt with "traditional" college educational system, i.e. attending classes on a local campus, the next chapter deals with the "non-traditional" method, including the important new eArmyU opportunity.

6

Nontraditional Education

Soldiers have many alternatives for gaining a professional base of knowledge. People generally think of the education process in terms of the traditional approaches available, such as colleges and vocational training programs. Although these avenues definitely represent legitimate ways of gaining an education, they do not always adequately serve the needs of the individual. Soldiers in particular often have unusual circumstances, such as frequent deployments, long or inconsistent work hours, and recurring permanent-change-of-station (PCS) moves. These obstacles often limit a soldier's ability to participate in the more traditional forms of education.

Obtaining a professional education should be viewed as a process in which several educational opportunities can be used to reach the overall goal. The philosophy behind nontraditional forms of education is that education is the goal, and methodology does not matter as much. The trick is to adequately prove that you have gained the necessary education.

As an example, assume that the skill to be learned is vehicle maintenance. There are several ways in which you could learn this skill. You might apply for an Army training course taught at an applicable service school, join a program at a well-known trade school, or request an apprenticeship. Or you may opt for a self-learning strategy in which you obtain professional reading materials and combine reading with practical experience. In reality, each of these methods will work.

DOCUMENTING THE LEARNING EXPERIENCE
Whichever method of gaining an education you choose, you need to properly document your learning experiences. In order to turn your nontraditional learning experiences into college transcripts, certificates, and diplomas—credentials that are readily accepted by the entire community of professionals—documentation is necessary.

INDEPENDENT OR DIRECTED-STUDY COLLEGE COURSES
Many colleges recognize that not everyone has the ability to attend college in a traditional classroom setting. Such colleges have self-study programs that

allow the student to meet the course learning objectives without attending class. As with a normal class setting, students are given a course syllabus that outlines the graded requirements and the due dates for each assignment. The student is usually given access to the course professor should he or she need any additional guidance.

The requirements vary greatly with each course. Some may require only reading and term papers; others may require periodic exams. These can be great courses, especially when used for subjects that do not require a lot of teacher attention, such as a history or humanities course. More technical courses, such as calculus or geometry, normally require more classroom-style explanation and often cannot be taken through independent study.

Self-study courses have the added benefit that the student can obtain a transcript from the school once the course is satisfactorily completed. The transcript can then be filed in the soldier's military record.

CABLE TELEVISION OR VIDEO COURSES

Taking college courses by viewing cable television or a video is very similar to the independent-study or directed-study courses, except that the professors' lectures are viewed outside of the normal classroom. In both cases, students are able to listen to classroom instruction in the comfort of their living rooms. Cable network classes use local television stations to broadcast lectures. The class syllabus normally gives the viewing times available for each of the class lectures. Often, classes are rebroadcast several times so that students can pick the most convenient program for their schedules. Students also can record the lectures themselves as they are aired and view the lecture at a later time. Video courses work much the same way, except that the lectures are prerecorded and loaned out to the students when they sign up for the course. This style of learning can be extremely helpful, because difficult subject matter can be viewed over and over again until adequately grasped. These courses also have the added advantage of existing under the umbrella of a traditional college or university.

ONLINE COURSES

A large number of students are attending college these days via online services. Even many of the more traditionally exclusive schools have opened up their campus doors to those who want to expand their horizons. Some of these courses can actually be paid for through tuition assistance dollars. Visit your local Education Center to see which courses are available through this form of nontraditional education, the newest of which is the eArmyU program.

LUNCHTIME, EVENING, OR NIGHT COLLEGE CLASSES

Particularly for the most difficult subject matter, it is often advantageous to participate in the traditional classroom setting. Many students find this the best option because of the group interaction found in many classrooms, as well educational credit, and operates several programs that assist agencies and institutions in providing recognition for skills, knowledge, and competencies gained through alternative means. Military members have benefited from the efforts of this coordinating body for more than fifty years. ACE is responsible for the evaluations of military training programs conducted through the service schools and similar training institutions. These evaluations have helped many soldiers receive college equivalent credit for their military training.

Evaluations are published in several ACE guides and are updated regularly. For soldiers, the most important of these guides is the *Guide to the Evaluation of Educational Experiences in the Armed Services*, which contains evaluations for military occupational specialty courses, basic training, NCOES courses, and many other formal courses offered by the Army, Army Reserve, and the Army National Guard. See the next page for a sample from this guide.

The Army/American Council on Education Registry Transcript System (AARTS)

AARTS is an automated system that is used for creating transcripts from military records of enlisted soldiers and some warrant officers. This database includes details of a soldier's military training and educational testing; this information is supplied to AARTS through several official sources. The unofficial transcripts on AARTS are designed to provide colleges and universities with an easy tool for determining credit awarded for military experience. The crediting recommendations are based on ACE guide evaluations, but the schools are not required to follow the recommendations. However, most postsecondary schools accept these recommendations and award civilian equivalent credit for these experiences.

Transcripts are available through the AARTS Operations Center. To request a transcript, fill out an application form (DD Form 295 or DA Form 5454-R) at your local Education Center. You also must submit a certified copy of your Personnel Qualifications Record (see your local Personnel Service Center). A sample AARTS transcript is available online at https://aarts.army.mil.

The same information can also be obtained through a Joint Services Transcript (JST) request. This service is available online at https://jst.doded.mil.

The eArmyU College Education Program

The Army recently launched an extensive online program called eArmyU, which makes postsecondary education available from virtually anywhere at any time. Under this umbrella, soldiers can obtain college degrees and have tuition costs covered in full. To qualify, Army enrollees must have at least three years' commitment remaining on their enlistment and agree to complete at least 12 semester hours of credit within a two-year period. (See the eArmyU Participation Agreement.) More information regarding this program is available at www.eArmyU.com.

as the availability of professor assistance. Fortunately, many college classes are available at lunchtime or after typical duty hours to meet even the most hectic schedules.

COLLEGE THROUGH CORRESPONDENCE

Like their military counterpart, college correspondence courses are an excellent resource for exportable education. It is possible to complete all of your degree requirements through correspondence courses. Numerous colleges offer extension programs or evaluation programs that accept this method of self-education.

Although some of these courses are completed in nearly the same manner as military courses, others require additional work. Typically, military courses are completed by passing an open-book examination provided at the back of the subcourse booklet. Many college correspondence courses require additional coursework, such as short term papers and writing projects. Some may even require closed-book examinations administered by a testing control officer on the installation.

Soldiers often prefer correspondence courses because they can be completed in any type of training environment. Even major deployments and similar field duty should not keep you from achieving your educational goals. Check with your local Education Center to find the most current programs available. Normally, tuition assistance is provided on a reimbursable basis for college correspondence course completion.

COLLEGE-LEVEL EQUIVALENCY EXAMINATIONS FOR CREDIT

Many college equivalency examinations, covering a wide range of topics and fields, are available to career-minded soldiers. These tests allow individuals to demonstrate that they have acquired the same level of knowledge that regular college students have in similar subjects. The tests can be used in a variety of ways. For instance, many soldiers use equivalency exams to verify personal experience or knowledge that is not documented elsewhere. Some soldiers find the tests useful as alternatives to the structured style of learning encountered in the classroom. These individuals often study subject matters on their own and then take the tests to validate their self-taught training.

Additionally, because the tests usually come from accredited institutions, many soldiers find equivalency exams very useful promotion tools. These official transcripts can be immediately placed in a soldier's personnel record and used for promotion credit. The tests count for the same credit as other college courses: 1 point for each semester hour earned. Common testing programs available to soldiers include the College-Level Examination Program (CLEP), Defense Activity for Non-Traditional Educational Support (DANTES), American College Testing Proficiency Examination Program (ACTPEP), Thomas Edison College Examination Program (TECEP), Regents College Examinations (RCE), and Graduate Record Examinations (GRE).

The following list gives some examples of individual exams that soldiers are often able to pass with no previous study. This list is definitely not complete and should be used only as a guide to stimulate further individual research.

Exam Title and Number	Source	Semester Hour Value
SP 562 Fundamentals of Counseling	DANTES	3
SE 532 Principles of Supervision	DANTES	3
SE 543 Introduction to Business	DANTES	3
SE 497 Introduction to Law Enforcement	DANTES	3
SD 539 Introduction to Management	DANTES	3
SE 756 Introduction to Carpentry	DANTES	3
SP 740 Basic Automotive Service	DANTES	3
SF 583 Beginning Spanish I	DANTES	3
SE 511 Environment and Humanity	DANTES	3
SD 457 History of West Civ to 1500	DANTES	3
SD 458 History of West Civ since 1500	DANTES	3
SE 424 Introductory College Algebra	DANTES	3
SE 821 Principles of Public Speaking	DANTES	3
SF 498 Criminal Justice	DANTES	3
SE 549 Basic Marketing	DANTES	3
SE 489 Foundations of Education	DANTES	3
SE 508 Here's to Your Health	DANTES	3
SF 531 Organizational Behavior	DANTES	3
SP 548 Money and Banking	DANTES	3
SE 935 Principles of Refrigeration	DANTES	3
American Literature	CLEP	3
Analysis & Interpretation of Literature	CLEP	3
English Literature	CLEP	3
Freshman English	CLEP	3
American Government	CLEP	3
American History to 1877	CLEP	3
American History 1865–Present	CLEP	3
Human Growth & Development	CLEP	3
Introductory Macroeconomics	CLEP	3
Introductory Microeconomics	CLEP	3
Introductory Sociology	CLEP	3
College Algebra	CLEP	3
General Biology	CLEP	3
General Chemistry	CLEP	3
Info Systems & Computer Applications	CLEP	3
Introduction to Management	CLEP	3
Introductory Accounting	CLEP	3

All of these tests have practice pretests available through the testing a cies and other related organizations. A score of 75 percent or better or pretest would probably translate into a passing score on the actual test. Ger CLEP tests also are available in broader areas of study, such as humani social sciences and history, English, mathematics, and the natural sciences, are worth 6 semester hours of credit each.

Choosing Equivalency Tests Wisely

Equivalency tests make good sense for many soldiers. Most education c selors encourage soldiers to start an individual study program by taking sev of these tests. Usually the target tests are the general CLEP exams, because Education Centers and post libraries often have a lot of study material to soldiers prepare for these tests. Soldiers have been successfully taking t exams for a long time with good results. The only drawback is that most diers will have to invest several weeks of study time in order to pass mos the general CLEP exams. This is still faster than attending college, though, has the advantage of being cost-free. In addition, you can study for these t around any work schedule.

Be wise, however, about which exams you decide to challenge. Study for one general CLEP exam may take you the same amount of time as it wo to take and pass several individual exams. The best strategy is to go to your l Education Center and review all the tests available. Take pretests in every that you think you might have some innate skill. Some of the results might prise you. Then schedule and take each test for which you scored 75 percen above on the pretest. If you do not pass the test but are close to achieving a p ing score, spend a couple days reviewing the subject matter and then try aga

If you speak a foreign language, you can potentially earn up to 18 cre hours by passing the foreign language examinations. This is a wonderful v for soldiers whose second language is English to take advantage of their ab ties in their native language.

WHAT TO EXPECT FROM AN ARMY EDUCATION COUNSELOI

Education counselors working in Army Education Centers or Army Learni Centers should be able to provide information and assistance on soldier car paths and methods of improving individual competencies. They can provi advice on college attendance, career choices, vocational programs, testing, f eign languages, tuition assistance, GI Bill benefits, and alternative funds college. They should be able to help with all of your educational goals.

COLLEGE CREDIT FOR YOUR MILITARY EXPERIENCE

The American Council on Education (ACE) is a nationally recognized coord nating body for postsecondary education (education beyond high school This council develops and influences credentialing guidelines, recommen

Location: Logistics Management Center, Ft. Lee, VA.

Length: Average 4 weeks.

Exhibit Dates: 7/77–12/88.

Objectives: To provide personnel with an overview of the Army wholesale logistics system and to develop managerial skills.

Instruction: Correspondence lessons cover life-cycle material management, procurement, functional management of assets, information concepts for managers, management theory and decision making, quantitative techniques, working capital funds, and an introduction to defense financial management.

Credit Recommendation: In the upper-division baccalaureate category, 4 semester hours in basic materiel systems management (3/78).

AR-0326-0041

ADMINISTRATIVE SYSTEMS ANALYSIS AND DESIGN

Course Number: RM409.

Location: Seventh Army Combined Arms Training Center, Munich, Germany; On-site other European locations.

Length: 2 weeks (78–80 hours).

Exhibit Dates: 6/79–7/80.

Objectives: To provide students with the principles and techniques employed in analyzing, evaluating, improving, and designing effective administrative systems to support management policy and decision making.

Instruction: Lecture conferences and group and individual practical exercises to cover an introduction to administrative systems, systems analysis, flow chart procedures, forms and report analysis and design, various automated systems, planning for systems, role of manager and analyst, and a major analysis and design project of a current management problem.

Credit Recommendation: In the lower-division baccalaureate/associate degree category, 3 semester hours in office management (9/80).

AR-0326-0042

ARMY MEDICAL DEPARTMENT OFFICER ADVANCED

Course Number: 6-8-C22.

Location: Academy of Health Sciences, Ft. Sam Houston, TX.

Length: 20 weeks (569 hours).

Exhibit Dates: Version 1: 6/90–Present. Version 2: 6/87–5/90.

Learning Outcomes: Upon completion of the course the student will have acquired general and specific advanced level military education and training. The AMEDD officer will be prepared to take command, leadership and staff positions of greater responsibility.

Instruction: Lectures, seminars, conferences, demonstrations and practical exercises with particular emphases on military science topics and health care administration. Students attend a common core, then subject-specific tracks.

Credit Recommendation: Version 1: Pending evaluation. Version 2: In the upper-division baccalaureate category, 9 semester hours in business management and organization (4/88).

AR-0326-0044

MASTER PLANNER

Course Number: EH 456.

Location: Combined Arms Training Center, Vilseck, W. Germany.

Length: 2 weeks (80 hours).

Exhibit Dates: 4/81–Present.

Learning Outcomes: Upon completion of the course, the student will be able to make limited studies in technical areas; coordinate information and approvals required to prepare a master plan; develop documents of the master plan, including environmental impact, land use, general site, utilities, road networks and technical support services; define functional requirements as Military Construction Army (MCA) programming; provide MCA details regarding cost estimates, construction criteria, energy requirements, and equipment programming; provide justification paragraphs and site sketches.

Instruction: Demonstrations, conference classes and practical exercises in the techniques, policies, and documents necessary for master planning considerations and construction planning. Main topics include development of a master plan to include documents, articulation with a community planning board, construction planning, and cost estimating.

Credit Recommendation: In the upper-division baccalaureate category, 1 semester hour in project management and 1 in community planning (10/88).

AR-0326-0045

MANPRINT STAFF OFFICERS

Course Number: 7C-F27/500-F18.

Location: Humphreys Center, Ft. Belvoir, VA; Soldier Support Center, Ft. Belvoir, VA; Xerox Center, Leesburg, VA.

Length: 2–3 weeks (117 hours).

Exhibit Dates: 10/87–Present.

Learning Outcomes: Upon completion of the course, the student will be able to introduce human factors engineering considerations into the management of a material development and acquisition process in order to increase performance in the total system.

Instruction: Includes classroom instruction, practical exercises, and independent study in the issues of manpower management, personnel, training, safety, human performance and workload analysis, and their effect on an acquisition system.

Credit Recommendation: In the upper-division baccalaureate category, 2 semester hours in organizational behavior (with an emphasis on the non-theoretical approach) (12/88).

AR-0326-0046

ORGANIZATIONAL DEVELOPMENT CONSULTANTS

Course Number: ODCC 1-90.

Location: Professional Education Center, Cp. Joseph Robinson, North Little Rock, AR.

Length: 15 weeks (579 hours).

Exhibit Dates: 9/88–Present.

Learning Outcomes: Upon completion of the course, the student will be able to directly apply negotiation and consulting skills in accomplishing organizational objectives.

Instruction: Instruction includes lecture, practical experience, structual experience, objective examination, discussion, reports, student demonstration, team development and feedback to individuals.

Credit Recommendation: In the upper-division baccalaureate category, 3 semester hours in human resources management consulting (7/90).

AR-0326-0047

LOGISTICS MANAGEMENT DEVELOPMENT

Course Number: 8A-F16.

Location: Army Logistics Management College, Ft. Lee, VA; Army Logistics Management College, Onsite locations, Continental US.

Length: 4 weeks (152–153 hours).

Exhibit Dates: 1/89–Present.

Learning Outcomes: Upon completion of the course, the student will be able to explain the fundamental concepts of materiel development and apply specific logistics policies and procedures; define and use the life-cycle management model in the contracting, inventory management, distribution, maintenance, and disposal of materiel; use statistical and probability techniques, computer tools, and behavioral theory to solve logistics problems; and integrate financial management theory into logistics operations.

Instruction: Lectures, discussions, and simulation exercises. Topics include life-cycle management model, contracting, materiel readiness, asset management, financial management, and specific decision-making tools.

Credit Recommendation: In the upper-division baccalaureate category, 4 semester hours in logistics management (10/91).

AR-0326-0048

LOGISTICS MANAGEMENT DEVELOPMENT BY CORRESPONDENCE

Course Number: 8A-F16.

Location: Army Logistics Management College, Ft. Lee, VA.

Length: Maximum 52 week.

Exhibit Dates: 1/89–Present.

Learning Outcomes: Upon completion of the course, the student will be able to explain the fundamental concepts of materiel development and apply specific logistics policies and procedures; define and use the life-cycle management model in the contracting, inventory management, distribution, maintenance, and disposal of materiel; use statistical and probability techniques, computer tools, and behavioral theory to solve logistics problems; and integrate financial management theory into logistics operations.

Instruction: This is a correspondence course. Topics include life-cycle management model, contracting, materiel readiness, asset management, financial management, and specific decision-making tools.

Credit Recommendation: In the upper-division baccalaureate category, 4 semester hours in logistics management (10/91).

AR-0326-0049

ARMY MAINTENANCE MANAGEMENT

Course Number: 8A-F3.

Location: Army Logistics Management College, Ft. Lee, VA; Army Logistics Management College, Onsite locations, Continental US.

Length: 4 weeks (152 hours).

Exhibit Dates: 8/89–Present.

Learning Outcomes: Upon completion of the course, the student will be able to increase

AGREEMENT

This Agreement between the undersigned Soldier and the U.S. Army contains the terms and conditions of the eArmyU program. In exchange for tuition and technology package (laptop), the Soldier agrees to complete the specified semester hours (SH) within the required period and meet criteria for program eligibility as defined by senior leadership. Soldiers may be required to reenlist or extend for duty in the U.S. Army to meet the 36-month service remaining requirement (SRR).

1. ELIGIBILITY

Regular active duty enlisted Soldiers who meet the enrollment eligibility criteria as defined by senior Army leadership, may be eligible to enroll. Certain grades of regular active duty enlisted Soldiers will be targeted by senior Army leadership. Soldier must have a high school diploma or GED certificate. **Soldier incurs a 36-month (SRR) upon enrollment in the eArmyU program in accordance with AR 601-280.** The SRR begins from the unit commander's signature date (CSD) on this eArmyU Participation Agreement. Soldier must receive approval from the unit commander and a Department of Army Education Services Specialist (ESS)/Counselor who will counsel Soldier regarding the special considerations involved in online distance learning (DL) and approve program enrollment. At the time program enrollment is activated on the eArmyU portal, the Soldier may enroll in eArmyU courses. This form must be processed and returned to the Education Center within 30 days from the date of counselor's signature.

2. TUITION ASSISTANCE

The Army will pay 100% of Soldier's eArmyU tuition assistance (TA) (includes tuition, books, fees, academic tutoring, program mentoring, Helpdesk and Internet access; does not cover commercial telephone service for Internet access) up to the established annual tuition ceiling and per-semester-hour tuition cap. **The first year tuition ceiling will be reduced by the cost of the laptop.** eArmyU tuition is only authorized for courses required for the completion of Soldier's approved educational plan in accordance with AR 621-5. The use of eArmyU TA is authorized for courses leading to the successful completion of 12 SH within the milestone date (36 months). Thereafter, TA is authorized on a course by course basis subject to the availability of funding. Soldiers who are sent course materials and who drop courses 11 or fewer days prior to course start date will be required to reimburse the Army a portion of the obligated tuition. (For example, ten or fewer days prior to course start date = 18% tuition reimbursement; between 1% to 6% of the course length = 35% tuition reimbursement; between 7% to 13% of the course length = 56% tuition reimbursement; between 14% to 19% of the course length = 75% tuition reimbursement; 20% or more of the course length = 100% tuition reimbursement).

3. CONTRACTUAL REENLISTMENT SERVICE OBLIGATION/SRR AND CORRESPONDING REIMBURSEMENT

Soldier enrolled in eArmyU is liable for eArmyU tuition cost of successfully completed courses for the duration of the Soldier's SRR. **Soldier may not voluntarily withdraw from eArmyU, may not return the laptop, and is responsible for the security of the laptop and virus protection of the laptop operating system. Upon successful completion of 12 SH of eArmyU coursework, Soldier assumes full ownership of the laptop.** Soldier commits to a 36-month SRR and must successfully complete a minimum of 12 semester hours (SH) of eArmyU coursework within 36 months from the date the technology package is issued. If Soldier fails to successfully complete 12 SH in 36 months from the date the technology package is issued, Soldier will be required to reimburse the Government a prorated portion of the cost of the technology package. The prorated reimbursement will be based on the percentage of SH (out of 12) NOT successfully completed in 36 months. This percentage will be multiplied by the actual dollar value of the eArmyU laptop. (For example, Soldier completes only 9 SH in 36 months. Soldier fails to complete 3 SH or 25 % of the required 12 SH [3/12 = 25%]. If laptop costs $1299.00, 25% = $324.75 reimbursement required.)

If eligible to enroll in eArmyU, as determined by paragraph 1 above, Soldier affirms that he/she has the retainability to complete the course within the institution-stipulated enrollment period and does not expect to be involuntarily separated. If notified of involuntary separation, Soldier will notify the ACES Counselor immediately. Voluntary requests for separation or retirement prior to the expiration of the SRR require additional approval. Regular active duty will seek additional approval through commander who will forward request to U.S. Army Human Resources Command (AHRC-PDT-PM). If approved to separate or retire before the SRR is complete, Soldier must repay the Government a prorated portion of the cost of eArmyU tuition for courses successfully completed. The amount of tuition to repay is based on the unserved portion of the SRR. If approved to separate or retire before the SRR is complete, Soldier is also responsible for the cost of the Laptop as stated in this agreement. Recoupment amount is calculated by dividing the amount of eArmyU tuition for successfully completed courses by the total SRR of 36 months and then multiplying times the number of months remaining before the SRR is met. For example, if Soldier has served 12 months of a 36-month SRR and has 24 months of service remaining and has successfully completed 6 SHs of eArmyU coursework at a total cost to the Army of $1,800.00, divide the Army's cost of successfully completed courses ($1,800.00) by 36 months and then multiply by 24 months = $1,200.00 recoupment required.

eArmyU Participation Agreement

Soldier who is subsequently commissioned as an officer/warrant officer may remain in eArmyU laptop option up to the 36 monthsfrom the date the technology package is received or until the required 12 SH are successfully completed, whichever comes first, subject to the terms and conditions and corresponding reimbursement requirements stipulated above. Thereafter commissioned officers/warrant officers are eligible for TA on a course-by-couse basis subject to availability of funding.

4. COURSE REQUIREMENT

Soldier will be subject to reimbursement to the Army for the entire amount of eArmyU TA received if the Soldier fails/withdraws/fails to complete an eArmyU course for academic or personal reasons. This includes: receipt of "F" for failure to participate or maintain contact with the instructor; failure to remove an incomplete grade within 120 days; failure to maintain a grade point average (GPA) of 2.0 after 15 SH, or thereafter, using TA; withdrawal for personal reasons; or withdrawal due to official separation, confinement, or similar administrative action by the Soldier's unit commander for disciplinary or fraudulent causes. Regardless of the reason, Soldier will advise Education Center of any intent to withdraw from a course covered by TA.

Reimbursement for course withdrawal may be waived, as verified by Soldier's unit commander. If extenuating circumstances prevent successful completion (e.g., deployments, emergency leave, death of a family member, illness/hospitalization). Solider must process a request for reimbursement waiver due to military reasons in the portal prior to the course end date. Requests for withdrawal due to military reasons require verification by the unit commander and the first Lieutenant Colonel in Soldier's chain of command. Fradulent waiver requests will be subject to UCMJ action. **If the cap or the annual tuition ceiling is reached and Soldier uses any other payment source for tuition costs, only the Army portion is subject to reimbursement.**

5. ESTIMATED FIRST-YEAR FINANCIAL COMMITMENT OF SOLDIER (Note that tuition costs, books and fees vary by school, course and degree/certificate level. Estimate 4 SH for first 12 months.)

_____ + _____ _____
    Tuition/books/fees   Technology package cost (laptop)   TOTAL ESTIMATED COST

6. SOLDIER'S AGREEMENT

I CERTIFY THAT I HAVE CAREFULLY READ THIS AGREEMENT AND UNDERSTAND ALL BENEFITS AND OBLIGATIONS I INCUR AS A RESULT OF ENROLLMENT IN eArmyU. I CERTIFY THAT I MEET ALL THE REQUIREMENTS FOR ENROLLMENT IN eArmyU, AS STATED IN THIS AGREEMENT AND AS VERIFIED BY MY SIGNATURE AND INITIALS BELOW. IF I NO LONGER MEET THE CONDITIONS TO PARTICIPATE IN eArmyU AFTER THE TIME THIS SIGNED AGREEMENT IS RETURNED TO THE EDUCATION CENTER OR PRIOR TO MY ENROLLMENT IN eArmyU, I UNDERSTAND THAT THIS AGREEMENT WILL BE NULL AND VOID AND I WILL BE RESPONSIBLE FOR REIMBURSEEMENT OF TA AND COSTS IF/AS APPLICABLE. **I UNDERSTAND THIS PARTICIPATION AGREEMENT MUST BE RETURNED TO THE EDUCATION CENTER WITHIN 90 DAYS FROM DATE OF COUNSELOR'S SIGNATURE.**

a. SOLDIER'S PRINTED NAME (Last, First, Middle Initial)	b. SSN
c. SIGNATURE	d. DATE

7. ARMY ESS/COUNSELOR APPROVAL

Soldier has been counseled regarding the terms and conditions of the eArmyU program.
I (initial one of the following options):

_____ Approve Soldier request for participation

_____ Disapprove. Soldier needs further preparation for DL

a. COUNSELOR'S PRINTED NAME (Last, First, Middle Initial)	b. DUTY PHONE/E-MAIL
c. SIGNATURE	d. DATE

eArmyU Participation Agreement *continued*

8. COMMANDER'S SUPPLEMENTAL AGREEMENT

This agreement serves to apprise the commander of the requirements of the eArmyU program and the conditions that support successful completion of the goals of the program.

a. The following are basic conditions required for participation in eArmyU:

Soldier must reenlist for duty in combat forces/operational units as defined by senior Army leadership, subject to adjustment, which is verified by Career Counselor/Reenlistment NCO at the bottom of this form.

Soldier incurs a 36-month SRR from the CSD on the eArmyU Participation Agreement and agrees to successfully complete 12 SH of eArmyU coursework within 36 months.

Soldier must be eligible for favorable personnel action.

Soldier must be counseled by an Army ESS/counselor who determines Soldier's potential for success in eArmyU and approves or disapproves Soldier's participation. Commander will verify Army ESS/counselor section approval is complete prior to completing and signing commander's section _____ (Commander's initials). Soldier must have joint approval by unit commander and Army ESS/Counselor to participate in eArmyU.

b. Commander agrees to support Soldier's academic pursuits with an understanding of the following:

Soldier incurs a financial obligation if the goals of the program are not met in the stipulated time frame. Army incurs the financial obligation for tuition/fee payment to academic institutions when unit commander approves failure/withdrawal/incomplete due to military reasons. _____ (Commander's initials)

c. Commander's Approval (initial one line below as applicable)

I fully understand the specific conditions of eArmyU enrollment and upon approval will support this Soldier's participation and will monitor his/her progress to ensure successful completion of program goals.

_____ (1) Approved. Soldier meets all conditions for eArmyU participation as listed in section 8 above, defined by senior Army leadership and has secured approval for enrollment from Army ESS/Counselor. Soldier referred to servicing Career Counselor to satisfy completion of section 9 of this agreement.

_____ (2) Disapproved. Soldier request for participation is disapproved.

a. COMMANDER'S NAME, RANK AND BRANCH	b. SIGNATURE	d. DATE

9. CAREER COUNSELOR'S/REENLISTMENT NCO CONCURRENCE

Soldier has reenlisted for duty in combat forces/operational units as defined by senior Army leadership, subject to adjustment, as verified below for participation in the eArmyU program. Certain grades of regular active duty enlisted Soldiers are targeted to participate in eArmyU, as defined by senior Army leadership, subject to adjustments. The Soldier's reenlistment, as defined by senior Army leadership, under the terms of this PA is: _____ Soldier's new ETS date is: _____
(DD Form 4 or DA Form 1695 is attached).

a. COUNSELOR'S PRINTED NAME (Last, First, Middle Initial)	b. SIGNATURE	d. DATE

eArmyU Participation Agreement *continued*

TIPS ON DOCUMENTING YOUR MILITARY EXPERIENCE
FOR COLLEGE CREDIT

Your military experience has an incredible amount of potential for earning you college course equivalency. Many soldiers, however, experience difficulty in finding ways to transfer those skills to a civilian education transcript. Reasons for this may include inexperience in dealing with colleges, undocumented experience, missing records and misinformation, and inaccurate transfer documentation by the colleges. Solving these problems can often translate into the addition of several college credits.

Success in college credit awards begins with good documentation of your past work and vocational or training experience. The majority of your military experience can be readily documented because it can be retrieved from your Personnel Qualifications Record (2-1), military orders, or a DD Form 214, Discharge Certificate.

Another step in the documentation process is to systematically diagram each year of your life since high school. Some high school students are given vocational training in certain areas, which may qualify for transfer credit. You should have kept adequate records of classes, courses, and training received. Closely examine each year to ensure that nothing worth potential credit is overlooked. This is particularly important if you have held multiple MOSs, taken other courses, or been in military service for several years.

Once you have collected all of the supporting documents, it's time to visit the local Education Center and fill out a request form for an Army/ACE Registry Transcript (AART) or Joint Services Transcript (JST). These are probably the best documents to present to colleges when arguing for equivalent military experience credit, because they relieve the colleges of having to use the ACE guide themselves. The ACE guide is a very good resource book, but the courses are often difficult for counselors to find. Even colleges that frequently deal with military personnel sometimes have a hard time locating course descriptions and MOS material.

Additionally, do not be afraid to ask the college counselor and his or her supervisor about other options for proving your proficiency. You may be allowed to demonstrate subject matter proficiency verbally to a professor in your field of knowledge. The college may have an in-house test that you can take to prove your skill.

You may have other experiences that are just as valuable but that are not listed on any standard personnel documents. For example, you may have been a training room clerk or worked in the Personnel Actions Center (PAC) for several years and yet were never awarded an MOS or additional skill identifier (ASI). This experience can still count if you can document it in some fashion. If you were rated in the job, the EER, SEER, or NCOER may be the ticket to some extra credit. Certificates of course completion or past SQT or SDT scores may prove valuable as well.

(Letterhead)

(Office Symbol)   (Date)

MEMORANDUM FOR: Registrar's Office, College Name, Address

SUBJECT: Military Credit Evaluation for SGT Smith

1. SGT Smith is facing a critical military promotion and needs additional civilian transcript credit in order to improve his promotion potential. For this reason, I am asking the college to evaluate SGT Smith's military credit and add it to his transcript. He has attended several military schools that have been recommended by the American Council on Education for equivalent civilian college credit.

2. He had his military experience evaluated onto an AARTS transcript in July of 2003. Since then, he has attended another course (BNCOC) and been promoted to SGT (he was a specialist when he had the previous evaluation completed). The ACE guide normally gives more weight and credit to the NCO ranks. We are including current pages from the ACE guide that show the evaluation weight given to this higher rank. Supporting documentation is also included.

3. Please consider using the full ACE guide recommendations. SGT Smith realizes that some of the recommended credit may not actually apply to a particular degree program. Transcripted credit from an accredited college and/or university is recognized for promotion point evaluations regardless of its value in degree completion.

4. Thank you very much for your courteous assistance on behalf of one of our soldiers. If you need any additional information, please feel free to call me at (012) 345-6789.

                                        Commander's Name
                                        Rank, Branch
                                        Commanding

Sample Letter Requesting Full Credit for Military Experience

If you can't obtain documentation, the best approach is to find a resource that already outlines those skills and use it as a guide in your request for credit. One great source is AR 611-201, Enlisted Career Management Fields and Military Occupational Specialty, which contains the classifications for MOSs for the current enlisted and officer career fields. Use it to find the scope and duties of practically every job in the Army environment. Then direct a letter to the college, using the MOS descriptions to outline the applicable training you received, the scope of the duties, and the time period covered. Make the argument as specific as possible to the experience received. For instance, you may have learned how to type or edit documents, or learned a computer program. By submitting your own documentation outlining these skills, a college may recognize them for credit.

If the college refuses to grant all of the credit recommended by the American Council on Education, this can be a formidable problem to overcome. College counselors may recommend that a soldier choose a two-year degree program rather than a four-year program. The broader four-year plans usually allow for more transfer credit, regardless of whether a soldier intends to finish the complete program. In other words, a soldier can lose the potential of earning transfer credit simply by choosing his or her degree program unwisely.

Make sure the institution does not skip credit because of the lower-division or upper-division recommendation shown in the ACE guide. If you are seeking a degree from a two-year college, the college may be ignoring recommended upper-division credit unnecessarily. The reverse argument is also true for four-year colleges. Accreditation standards allow for these differences between programs, and their particular constraints shouldn't limit the transfer of your credit. Also, be aware of the possibility that your AART transcript may not be complete. Some soldiers' backgrounds should be handled jointly by a DD Form 295 or a DA Form 5454-R and an AART transcript. Your local Education Center can provide you with all of these.

College transfer credit policies vary widely, and because taking classes at one college usually does not prohibit you from also taking classes elsewhere, it may be in your best interest to participate in more than one college program in order to maximize your transfer credit. Military experience may be more readily accepted at one school than another and once it is on that college's transcript, it may be more easily transferred to other, more reluctant colleges. Refer to the sample letter as a guide for substantiating requests for full credit.

PART III

Progression
to the Officer Ranks

7

Warrant Officer Selection

The warrant officer field is a great career progression move for soldiers with the right combination of skills, motivation, and background. Be warned, however, that this path will take you into a world of stiff competition and high expectations. Warrant officers are expected to be the "technocrats" in their fields. They are the leaders that solve the majority of the tough technical problems. Most warrant fields demand broad field experience and plenty of technical schooling. It is a good career move for many talented enlisted and noncommissioned officers. Most warrants come from the NCO ranks, where they have had several years of experience working in their fields. Most are from maintenance or related logistical backgrounds and support the repair and upkeep of the military's equipment.

This chapter is not designed to cover every possible warrant officer procurement possibility, but rather intended to give you the background you need to put together a successful warrant officer packet, regardless of which avenue you choose. Most of the pieces in this packet are generic and are required of every potential candidate for warrant officer. Use the information and the sample letters in this chapter as a guide for your own specific track.

WARRANT OFFICER TRAINING AND CAREER POTENTIAL

If you are selected to be a warrant officer, you will be required to attend the Warrant Officer Candidate School at Fort Rucker, Alabama. This six-week course is extremely challenging and is designed to test your mental and physical capacities. Upon graduation from this course, you will be commissioned as a WO1 with a follow-on assignment to the Warrant Officer Basic Course for your career management field. Most new warrants are assigned to field units after completing their Basic Course. You will be expected to become a subject matter expert in your field and will be evaluated accordingly.

Career progression opportunities are very good for warrant officers. Most can expect to make CW3 before retirement, with many going on to make CW4. The absolute best may be asked to extend their careers to pin on the newest warrant officer rank of CW5.

WARRANT OFFICER SELECTION CRITERIA

Selection as a warrant officer in today's Army depends not only on how qualified you are as a soldier, but also on how well you present those qualifications to the Centralized Warrant Officer Selection Board. Warrant officer candidates' records are reviewed at the Department of the Army level, with selections being made for the varied fields of service. The board members are given the task of selecting only the best-qualified applicants for the limited slots within the Army's warrant officer structure. There are no local boards to go through except personal interviews with commanders within the soldier's chain of command. By far the most critical part of the whole process is the packet itself, because it represents the only you that the Centralized Board will ever see. Your packet must be strong, with any problem areas carefully explained or eliminated by waiver, before final submission to the Centralized Board.

There are areas that are definitely key to your packet's success. First, you have to have strong report cards. If you are an NCO, the board will look at your entire file, with specific interest given to the most recent five years. Every packet requires endorsements from your chain of command, normally through and including the brigade commander. These recommendations are very important and carry significant weight in the eyes of the board members, because they often offer the most credible evidence that you have the potential for success in this more challenging role.

The Warrant Officer Procurement Program is outlined in DA Circular 601-99-1 and DA Pamphlet 601-110. The procurement process is constantly undergoing change and you should visit your installation warrant officer procurement representative to get the latest information. This office is usually affiliated with the Personnel Services Branch.

The eligibility criteria are specific for each specialty, but waivers can be granted for most requirements. All warrant officer applicants must have a minimum GT score of 110, which is unwaiverable. If your GT score is lower than 110, make arrangements with your local Education Center to implement an improvement program. Most installations now have self-paced, computer-based improvement programs. If you took your GT test a long time ago when in high school, you may want to retest. Many soldiers score much better a few years later after they have gained experience and maturity. This is definitely a route to consider if your previous score is close to the 110 requirement. The standard of error for the GT score is 3 to 6 points, and this may be all the improvement you need. Check with your education counselor.

Almost all warrant officer selections are made from enlisted feeder military occupational specialties, which are those enlisted MOSs that provide the background necessary to begin the technical career mandates of a particular warrant officer specialty. Not all enlisted MOSs feed warrant officer specialties. The exception is rotary wing aviator (153A); for these helicopter pilot positions, all enlisted soldier MOSs are considered possible feeder MOSs because all of their training and technical knowledge is within the aviation arena. The physical standards are much higher for aviation warrants because of the inherent risks involved in flying aircraft. Usually only soldiers possessing perfect twenty-twenty vision are allowed to compete for these slots. Check with your local representative, though, as these guidelines are always subject to change based on the needs of the Army.

Some enlisted MOSs feed several warrant officer specialties. If this is true for you, then you may want to submit a separate packet for each warrant officer specialty. This is an important step, as you may be fully qualified to become a warrant in a particular field, but if no positions are available within that specialty you will not be picked up. Make sure each packet can stand alone on its own merits and that it is individually directed toward the needs of the specialty requested. Different aspects of your background may be emphasized or deemphasized based on the requirements of each specialty. For example, if you are a Patriot missile operator and mechanic (24T MOS), you could feed into one of the following five warrant officer specialties: Hawk system technician (140D), Patriot system technician (140E), command and control systems technician (140A), forward area air defense systems technician (140B), or rotary wing aviator (153A). See the sample Warrant Officer Checklist, page 94.

BOARD SELECTION CRITERIA
The criteria for selection are based on what the selection board is trying to create. First, consult the current DA Circular 601-99-1 and DA Pamphlet 601-110 to find out what specialties your MOS feeds. The circular is updated every two years and is your best reference tool for completing your warrant officer packet. Discovering what the board is looking for in each specialty is described very well in AR 611-112, Manual of Warrant Officer Military Occupational Specialties; your unit's orderly room should have a copy of it on file. The specialties are arranged in numerical order. All you have to do is look up each of the specialties that your MOS feeds and read the requirements. You will find that they are very specific and the verbiage is very clear. It is highly recommended that you consult this document while putting together your required professional résumé.

REQUESTING WAIVERS
What do you do if you find that your MOS does not feed to the warrant officer specialty you want? All is not lost. As they say in the Army, "Everything can be waivered, even the unwaiverable!" This is true for warrant officer specialties as well, although it is difficult. Your packet will have to be that much stronger in order to ask the Army to consider you above other highly credentialed soldiers from the correct feeder MOS. Do not be discouraged, though. There is a strategy for every obstacle.

You will have to start with a request for waiver of the feeder MOS requirement. This waiver request is nothing more than a letter from you to the board outlining your argument for a favorable response. Your argument should include strong reasoning and have as many supporting documents as possible. A supporting document could be a letter from your commander or supervisor addressing some relevant skills that you have obtained through on-the-job-training. Better yet, it could be a certificate of completion from a training course at a military or civilian school. It could even be a correspondence course completion certificate stating that you have completed a nonresident course in the field covered by the warrant officer specialty.

Example of a Soldier Requesting a Waiver
Following is an example of a warrant officer specialty packet for a soldier who does not have the correct feeder MOS and who needs a strong argument in order to earn the warrant officer slot.

This candidate, SSG Doe, is a staff sergeant in a communications MOS (31R). She has a Patriot UHF Communications Operations Additional Skill Identifier (ASI) of X4, so she has a reasonable argument for her request to become a Patriot warrant officer. The 31R MOS is not a feeder MOS for anything except flight school. SSG Doe wears glasses and does not really have the credentials for pilot training, so this is her only hope for a possible warrant officer position. She is a stellar performer and has the records to prove it, including PT scores consistently above 270. She needs to convince the Army that her selection would be a smart move and well worth the additional training cost.

The first thing she needs to do is consult AR 611-112, Manual of Warrant Officer Military Occupational Specialties. This is very important, because this manual will provide SSG Doe with the minimum qualifications for the warrant specialty. The scope of duties is also listed, and that is where she will discover the strategy for writing a coherent argument for her packet. The qualifications are fairly standard and do not present any problems for SSG Doe. She is a US citizen and already has a secret clearance, which is required for her 31R MOS duties. Her vision is correctable and meets the requirements specified. She has full use of her hands, perfect hearing, and normal color vision. The only qualification lacking is the warrant officer school itself. The following list reflects the duties required by a Patriot missile system technician:

- Supervises unit maintenance and advises commander on Patriot system emplacement.
- Monitors equipment for operator error or system malfunctions.
- Instructs subordinates in procedures, maintenance techniques, and care of special tools.
- Evaluates maintenance program, trains operators, supervises repairs, and isolates faults.
- Directs shop operations, production control, shop supply, and parts exchanges.
- Implements quality control and proper safety and security measures.
- Advises commander on all maintenance and supply problems.
- Performs other essential duties that apply to the unit's mission.

Now SSG Doe needs to match up her background experience with these requirements. The sample waiver request shows what SSG Doe's argument might look like once her qualifications have been thoroughly analyzed and compared with the requirements.

The important lesson to learn from Doe's example is that you need to address how your background qualifies you for the warrant officer specialty you desire. Even if your credentials do not match as well as in this example, you may still have other qualifiers that would impress the board members.

It is also possible that the board may be looking for something other applicants do not have. Maybe the career field is critically short of warrants and your argument convinces the board that you are competitive. Whatever your shortfall, make sure you adequately address it in your packet; otherwise you will likely be considered unqualified. An approved waiver eliminates this packet problem.

LETTERS OF RECOMMENDATION

The letters of recommendation from your chain of command carry more weight than any other single item in the packet. Make sure that the letters in your packet present you in the most favorable light possible. They should be intelligently written to address the particular goal desired. Refer to the sample letter of recommendation as an example of one that might be found in a warrant officer packet.

HOW TO ADDRESS BACKGROUND PROBLEMS

What do you do if you have serious problems in your background? Does an Article 15 or a letter of reprimand that is filed in your permanent record automatically disqualify you from further advancement? This depends on whether you can prove that the negative information is behind you and will not adversely affect your future.

Another waiver will be required, but if you successfully obtain the waiver, there is the added benefit of leaving the past problems in your enlisted records behind. In this instance, there is an important rule about commissioned officer records that applies to warrant officer selectees. The Army has a policy of not looking at your enlisted file (except for security reasons) once you are picked up as an officer. This means that if you can persuade an officer selection board to pick you, then that negative blotch will no longer affect your career progression path. This is true for both warrant officers and commissioned officers. See page 92 for an example of a waiver request for a candidate with a prior Article 15 offense in his file.

As you can see in this sample waiver request, it is very important to outline the specific charges that were levied against you and how you may have grown from the incident. Be positive, and accept full responsibility for what you did in the past. For example, board members do not want to hear an excuse such as that the incident was caused by someone else. If a soldier accepted the Article 15, that is proof enough that the soldier was afforded the opportunity to clear himself at the time of the charge. If this applies to you, do not try to convince board members of your innocence ten years after the offense. Put it behind you and show them and the rest of the world that you truly have moved on.

(Letterhead)

(Office Symbol)   (Date)

MEMORANDUM FOR: COMMANDER, USAREC, Fort Knox, KY
                40121-2726

SUBJECT: Request for Waiver of Nonfeeder MOS Requirement for
         SSG Jane Doe

1. I am requesting a waiver for my nonfeeder MOS in order to meet
    the remaining requirements for my warrant officer packet. I have
    served over eight years in Patriot missile TO&E units alongside
    Patriot missile system operators and maintainers while serving in
    my 31R career field. My background is full of Patriot-specific knowl-
    edge that I have acquired through extensive cross-training.

2. My cross-training experiences have enabled me to learn the march
    order and emplacement requirements of the Patriot system. I have
    often been given leadership responsibility over my communications
    personnel as well as Patriot system mechanics and launcher crew
    members. I am very familiar with the Army Maintenance Manage-
    ment System (TAMMS), and I have completed PALS and ULLS
    computer system training.

3. Please give favorable consideration to this request. Our Patriot
    missile system technician, CW2 Anybody A. Warrant, is willing to
    verify my cross-training knowledge. He can be reached at DSN
    000-0000. Thank you for your favorable consideration of this
    request.

                            Jane Doe
                            SSG
                            Social Security Number

Waiver Example for Nonfeeder MOS

(Letterhead)

MEMORANDUM FOR: Department of the Army Warrant Officer
Selection Board

SUBJECT: Letter of Recommendation for SSG Jane Doe

1. SSG Jane Doe is a superb candidate for warrant officer selection. SSG Doe is one of those rare noncommissioned officers who automatically stands out from the crowd. She is undoubtedly one of the finest NCOs I have ever had the pleasure to work with. Her professional demeanor is such that other soldiers constantly seek to emulate her example.

2. SSG Doe has excelled in every aspect of military duty. Her technical competence and daily execution of duties are unparalleled. She has been pursuing her civilian education and has nearly completed her Bachelor of Arts degree. In addition, she was recently hand-picked by a Department of the Army review board for Drill Sergeant School.

3. She is also a dynamic soldier in the physical fitness arena. SSG Doe constantly scores above the 270 level on the PT test (most recently 299). Her enthusiasm during unit PT sessions is contagious and reflects highly on her personal commitment to excellence.

4. SSG Doe is a Patriot system operator and mechanic (24T) and wants to continue her professional career as a Patriot system warrant officer (140E). I believe she possesses the skills necessary to become an excellent warrant officer. Please do not miss this opportunity to add her name to the selection list for the next warrant officer candidate and 140E course slot.

5. Please feel free to call or write to me for any additional information. My office telephone number is DSN 000 000 or commercial (111) 123-2345/6789.

Commander's Name
CPT, Branch
Commanding

Sample Letter of Recommendation

(Letterhead)

(Office Symbol)   (Date)

MEMORANDUM FOR: Commander, USAREC,
                              Fort Knox, KY 40121-2726

SUBJECT: Request for Moral Waiver of Article 15 Received as a
                Private

1. Request a waiver for the Article 15 that I received as a private nine
    years ago. I was charged with an Article 92 violation, which was
    given to me for missing a required formation. My commander gave
    me fourteen days' extra duty and restriction and took one week's
    pay from me as punishment for my misconduct. The Article 15 pro-
    ceedings were held on 15 April 1996 at Fort Anywhere, Any State.

2. I regret having had this unfortunate incident and can only attribute
    it to my lack of maturity at the time. That Article 15 was an eye-
    opening experience for me and caused me to reexamine my
    lifestyle and make adjustments in my attitude and performance.

3. Since that time, I have done immeasurably well in the Army and
    have had no additional disciplinary problems. I have successfully
    competed for rank through SSG and was selected for NCO of the
    Quarter on two occasions. I have been pursuing my civilian educa-
    tion on my off-duty time and have completed 74 semester hours of
    college toward my degree goals. In addition, I have taken and com-
    pleted several correspondence course programs over the last few
    years.

4. Please forgive my past misconduct and do not allow this one mis-
    take to keep me from furthering my military career through selec-
    tion as a Patriot missile system warrant officer. My commander has
    agreed to provide any further evidence of my current duty perfor-
    mance. He can be reached at DSN 000-0000. Thank you for your
    assistance in this matter.

                                        Your Name
                                        Rank
                                        Social Security Number

Moral Waiver Example for Article 15 Offense

OTHER REQUIREMENTS FOR SELECTION

You now have the tools necessary to prepare a strong warrant officer selection packet. The packet is not exceptionally difficult to put together, as all requirements are self-explanatory and directed by DA Circular 601-99-1 and DA Pamphlet 601-110. You need to have a 110 GT score and get a security clearance of at least "secret" if you do not already have one. There are several standard form letters that you have to sign; these can simply be copied directly from the circular. A DA photo is required. Make sure your uniform is in excellent condition and fits you properly, and pay close attention to your awards and decorations and related items on the uniform; you do not want the board to get the wrong impression about you because of a minor oversight on your part. It goes without saying that you will have to be recommended by your chain of command.

Remember, the overall success of your packet is up to you. Many people will play a role in putting it together, but it is your packet. Make absolutely sure it presents the best image of you that the board could possibly see. Spend the time carefully typing each document, and have others evaluate the packet's contents. Seek out subject matter experts to help you reach your goals.

Warrant Officer Application Checklist

All documents should be single-sided copies and in the following order:

Name: _____

Board Packet (These copies should be clean and neat in appearance – they will make up your board packet being reviewed for your selection):

___ DA 61 (with HT/WT and APFT statement, signed as shown on the web site example)
___ Senior Warrant Officer Letter (Optional for some WOMOS)
___ Company Commander Letter of recommendation (or applicable Company Grade UCMJ authority)
___ Battalion Commander Letter of recommendation (or applicable Field Grade UCMJ authority)
___ Resume
___ ERB or equivalent document (used to verify DOB, GT, AFS, and ETS)
___ OMPF Hard Copies (Last three years of NCOERS and AERS in order newest to oldest)
___ College Transcript(s)
___ COPIES of Professional Certificates (Licenses or Certificates issued to Engineers, Mechanics etc…)
___ AFAST Results (153A applicants only)
___ DA Photo

Supporting Documents: (These documents are required to qualify your packet, but will not be reviewed by the board)

___ Security clearance (DO NOT SEND DA Form 873, minimum Interim Secret clearance required)
___ Physical Coversheet USAREC Form 1932 (Aviation - expires after 18 months, all others expire at 24 months. If waiver or exception to policy required, applicant needs to send complete physical. 153A applicants need to send DD 2808 with Stamp from USAAMC, Ft. Rucker)
___ DA Form 160-R enclosed (ensure that you sign it and block 9a is checked)
___ Remaining Hard Copy documents from OMPF not included on your ERB (awards, certificates)
___ Re-enlistment documents if ERB does not show 12 months remaining
___ Statement of understanding enclosed (a copy of this memo is on the web site)
___ Conditional Release enclosed if you are not an active duty Army applicant
___ English credit document if required (250N, 251A, 254A, 420A, 920A, 920B, 921A, 922A, 923A)
___ TABE score document if required (880A, 881A)
___ Body fat statement enclosed on DA 61 if required
___ Moral waiver request if required (as identified in blocks 26 on DA Form 61)
___ Age waiver request enclosed if required (max age is 33 for aviators, 36 for SF and 46 for all others)
___ Prerequisite waiver request enclosed if required (verify with MOS on web site)
___ AFS waiver request enclosed if required (12 years for all MOS)
___ APFT waiver request enclosed if required (must include Physical Profile and complete Physical with packet)
___ Checklist endorsed by PSB or S-1 NCO is acceptable (validating soldier is not flagged or barred)
___ Mail Completed Application to:

HEADQUARTERS US ARMY RECRUITING COMMAND
ATTN RCRO-SM-A
1307 THIRD AVENUE
FORT KNOX KY 40121-2725

This section to be completed and authenticated by PSD/MPD personnel or the Battalion S-1.

I certify that service member is not flagged and is eligible to apply for this program.

REVIEWER (printed name and title): _____
SIGNATURE: _____ DATE: _____
DSN PHONE #: _____COMM PHONE #: _____
EMAIL: _____

Packets can also be sent via Digital Sender to NewWarrantPackets@usarec.army.mil
Please follow up with the recruiting team to verify your packet was received.

8

Commissioned
Officer Selection

There are many fine soldiers in today's Army who would make excellent officers. The experience that prior service brings to the commissioned field is normally very good and can flavor the officer corps nicely. It is a challenging course, though, and far different from the NCO or enlisted way of life. Still, many find it a great career progression move and welcome the opportunity for further growth and development. There are many avenues open to soldiers for transitioning from the enlisted or noncommissioned ranks into the officer commissioning sources. There are three commissioning sources for officers: the Reserve Officers' Training Corps (ROTC), the US Military Academy at West Point, and Officer Candidate School (OCS). All of these sources provide the Army with many excellent young officers.

ROTC
The largest commissioning source is the Reserve Officers' Training Corps (ROTC), which trains officer cadets on college and university campuses around the country. ROTC is a four-year training program for college students and a two-year program for prior service soldiers with two years of college. You cannot remain on active duty and attend ROTC training. If you are currently on active duty, you can be released early from your current enlistment to join an ROTC-affiliated college under the Army's Green-to-Gold program. There are many scholarship opportunities available for qualified applicants that either pay for or help pay for your college tuition and related costs. There are opportunities for two-, three-, and four-year ROTC scholarships.

Soldiers with at least two years of college can qualify for entry into an advanced ROTC program. This level represents the last two years of the normal ROTC training program. They must have completed at least two years of their current active-duty enlistment, have at least a 2.5 grade point average, and have a letter of recommendation from their chain of command; they cannot be disqualified for commissioning for medical, security, or any other reason. Successful completion of the ROTC program does not guarantee an active-duty appointment. You may be commissioned into the Army Reserve or National Guard instead of the active Army (see DA Form 4824).

(Letterhead)

MEMORANDUM FOR: ROTC Program, Any College, USA

SUBJECT: Green-to-Gold Scholarship Recommendation for
        SGT Chambers

1. I am pleased to recommend SGT Chambers for a scholarship opportunity in the Army's Green-to-Gold program. SGT Chambers is an extremely faithful and tireless supporter of our unit's maintenance mission and is always motivated to accomplish any task given. He is ably qualified to finish his education and join the ranks of the Officer Corps.

2. SGT Chambers has the aptitude, integrity, and motivation to make an outstanding commissioned officer. Don't miss this opportunity to add another proven soldier to the proud lineage of ROTC scholarship officers.

3. Please feel free to call me at DSN 123-4567 or commercial (123) 456-7890 for any additional information or assistance in making his packet Green-to-Gold.

                             Commander's Name
                             CPT, Branch
                             Commanding

Sample Green-to-Gold Scholarship Recommendation

ADDENDUM TO CERTIFICATE AND ACKNOWLEDGEMENT OF SERVICE
REQUIREMENTS *(DA FORM 3540)* FOR ALL PERSONNEL APPLYING FOR PARTICIPATION IN THE RESERVE
OFFICERS TRAINING CORPS *(ROTC)*/SIMULTANEOUS MEMBERSHIP PROGRAM *(SMP)*
For use of this form, see AR 601-210; the proponent agency is DCS, G-1.

INFORMATION REQUIRED BY THE PRIVACY ACT

AUTHORITY:	Title 10 USC Section 270, 10 USC 511, 10 USC 673a and Executive Order 9397, 22 November 1943.
PRINCIPAL PURPOSE:	To explain additional obligations and participation requirements imposed as a result of this specific option and to insure that your agreement to these conditions is a matter of record.
ROUTINE USES:	Confirmation of obligations and participation requirements incurred under this option; occasionally as a basis for removal from the program if the requirements are not met.
DISCLOSURE:	Disclosure of your SSN is voluntary; however, if not provided you will not be accepted into the program.

APPLICABILITY

This addendum to DA Form 3540 will be completed by all individuals applying form participation in the ROTC/SMP and will be reproduced locally.

INSTRUCTIONS TO USAR ACCEPTANCE OFFICIAL

Each individual applying for participation in the ROTC/SMP will read, initial where indicated, and sign this addendum prior to participating in the program if they are currently unit members, or prior to being enlisted, reenlisted, extended, or reassigned, as a member of a troop program unit of the USAR. All questions will be answered to the applicant's satisfaction. After completion of the Authentication block below, a copy of this Addendum will be attached firmly to each copy of the DA Form 3540 and distributed in accordance with the instructions contained in Section IV, Chapter 8, AR 140-111.

EXPLANATION TO APPLICANT

1. In connection with my selection for participation in the ROTC/SMP as a currently assigned unit member, or in connection with my enlistment, reenlistment, extension of enlistment, or reassignment from Control Group *(ROTC)* to a troop program unit of the US Army Reserve, I accept the following

☐ Option 1: Selection for participation in ROTC/SMP as a member currently assigned to the appropriate troop program unit. I further acknowledge that *(check one)*:

☐ I have previously successfully completed a basic training course conducted by the US Armed Forces; or I have successfully completed 3 years or more of Junior ROTC and a letter of acceptance by a Professor of Military Science as credit placement for enrollment in Advanced ROTC has been issued and is available to the recruiting officials; or I have attended a Service Academy for one year; or I have successfully completed MS II; or I have successfully completed ROTC Basic Camp. Read and initial paragraphs 2a through 2f, h, i, j, l, and m.

☐ Entry on Initial Active Duty for Training *(IADT)* to complete basic training is required to be successfully completed prior to entrance in ROTC/SMP. Read and initial paragraphs 2a through 2f, h, i, j, l, and m.

☐ Option 2: Enlistment for ROTC/SMP with no previous military service or ROTC credit placement for enrollment in Advanced ROTC. Entry on Initial Active Duty for Training *(IADT)* to complete basic training is required to be successfully completed prior to entrance in ROTC/SMP. Read and initial paragraphs 2a through g, i, j, k, and m.

☐ Option 3: Enlistment, reenlistment, or extension of enlistment, for ROTC/SMP with one of the following:

    a. Previous military service and have successfully completed a basic training course conducted by US Armed Forces.

    b. Have successfully completed 3, or more, years of Junior ROTC and a letter of acceptance by a Professor of Military Science as credit placement for enrollment in Advanced ROTC, has been issued and is available to the recruiting officials.

    c. Have attended a Service Academy for one year.

    d. Have successfully completed MS II.

    e. Have successfully completed ROTC Basic Camp

Read and initial each paragraph 2 a through 2m.

☐ Option 4: Reassignment from Control Group *(ROTC)* to a troop program unit for participation in ROTC/SMP and already enrolled and participating in the Advanced ROTC Program. Read and initial paragraphs 2a, b, c, d, i, j, k, and m.

2. In connection with my enlistment, reenlistment, extension of enlistment, or reassignment from Control Group *(ROTC)* , the following additional agreements are acknowledged:

    a. I understand the ROTC/SMP is a voluntary officer training program which requires Reserve Component enlisted status for eligibility.

    b. I understand that by law *(10 USC 2106)* a commissioned officer may not apply credits which stem from enlisted service served concurrently with ROTC Advanced Course training, when computing length of service for any purpose.

    c. I understand that participants in the Army ROTC scholarship program are not eligible for participation in ROTC/SMP. ROTC/SMP participants may apply for Army ROTC scholarships; however, they will be reassigned from the troop program unit to the Control Group *(ROTC)* prior to acceptance of such scholarships.

    d. I agree that upon successful completion of the ROTC Advanced Course, to include ROTC Advanced Camp, I will volunteer for commissioning under the provisions of the ROTC Early Commissioning Program *(ECP)* if, upon completion, I am not scheduled to receive a baccalaureate degree within six months.

    e. I am not ineligible to enroll in the Advanced ROTC Program as provided in paragraph 3-14, AR 145-1.

DA FORM 4824, APR 2005   PREVIOUS EDITIONS ARE OBSOLETE.   APD V1.00

DA Form 4824

f. I understand if I am accepted for participation in the ROTC/SMP and do not apply for enrollment in the ROTC Advanced Course within one year following enlistment, I will be dropped as a potential ROTC/SMP participant and retained in the unit in an enlisted status until completion of my military service obligation *(statutory or contractual)*. I will also be required to undergo any initial active duty for training not previously completed.

g. I understand if I enlist directly for participation in the ROTC/SMP and I apply but am not accepted for enrollment in the ROTC Advanced Course *(see eligibility requirements, paragraphs 3 51 and 3-17, AR 145-1)* I will, at my request be retained in the unit, or be honorably discharged. If I am retained in an enlisted status I will be dropped as a potential ROTC/SMP participant and required to complete an initial active duty for training not previously completed.

h. I understand if I enlisted under any other enlistment program or option and was selected for ROTC/SMP participation and I do not apply for enrollment in the ROTC Advanced Course within one year following my selection, or I am not accepted for enrollment in the ROTC Advanced Course, I will be dropped as a potential ROTC/SMP participant and retained in an enlisted status until completion of my military service obligation *(statutory or contractual)*.

i. I understand that if I am disenrolled from Advanced ROTC, or fail to complete the ROTC Advanced Course, I will be dropped from the ROTC/SMP and, if otherwise qualified, retained in the unit in an enlisted status until completion of my military service obligation *(statutory or contractual)*. I must undergo initial active duty for training if not previously completed. I will be administratively reduced immediately to the grade and rank authorized by AR 140-158.

j. I understand that if I fail to volunteer for the ROTC Early Commissioning program *(ECP)*, or fail to accept a commission, or fail to be tendered a commission, I will be treated in the same manner as those ROTC/SMP participants who fail to complete Advanced ROTC. See paragraph i above.

k. I understand that when enlisting directly for participation in the ROTC/SMP I am not entitled to enlistment incentives under the provisions of DA Circular 135-23, or similiar Federal directives.

l. I understand that when entering the ROTC/SMP if I received an enlistment incentive under the provisions of DA Circular 135-23, or similiar Federal directives, I will not be entitled, upon my assignment to an officer-trainee position, to future incentive payments and may be required to pay back some, or all, of the money I have received prior to my assignment to an officer-trainee position.

m. I understand that any enlistment/reenlistment program, other than the Enlistment Incentive Program *(DA Circular 135-23, or other similiar Federal directives)*, which I would have otherwise elected and been eligible for upon initial enlistment/reenlistment, will be available upon my application for said program should I remain in an enlisted status upon removal from the ROTC/SMP.

3. I have read, initialed, and understood, each of the statements above which pertain to the option I chose in paragraph 1 above. Any other promise, representation, or commitment made to me in conjuction with my enlistment, reenlistment, extension of enlistment, or reassignment from Control Group (ROTC) , for participation in the Reserve Officers Training Corps *(ROTC)*/Simultaneous Membership Program *(SMP)* is written below in my own handwriting, or is hereby waived. *(If none, write "NONE".)*

AUTHENTICATION

ASSIGNED UNIT DESIGNATION AND COMPLETE ADDRESS *(Include ZIP Code)*

DATE	TYPED NAME AND SOCIAL SECURITY NUMBER OF APPLICANT	SIGNATURE OF APPLICANT
DATE	TYPED NAME, GRADE, BRANCH AND TITLE OF RECRUITING OFFICIAL	SIGNATURE OF RECRUITING OFFICIAL

DA FORM 4824, APR 2005

APD V1.00

DA Form 4824 *continued*

Officer training and selection programs are covered under AR 635-200 and AR 145-1. Each installation, participating colleges and universities, and most major cities have representatives who can help you complete an application packet. The sample letter is provided as a guide for recommendation to the Green-to-Gold scholarship program.

The soldier will also have to get a letter of acceptance from the professor of military science at the college offering the ROTC scholarship. In addition, he or she must have a minimum GT score of 115 and no more than ten years of active federal service. The scholarship application period usually starts in December and ends around 1 March of each academic year.

The ROTC scholarships do not affect your other education benefits earned while on active-duty status. The Green-to-Gold program is an excellent way for qualified soldiers to achieve career-progression goals through commissioned service. Competition is tough, but the rewards are high and the challenges exciting.

WEST POINT AND WEST POINT PREP SCHOOL

The second commissioning source to explore is the US Military Academy at West Point. This is probably one of the finest military schools in the world and is known for its quality education. This outstanding education costs the military a great deal of money and costs you a lot of hard work amid stiff competition. The West Point tradition is a long-standing one, dating back to 1802. There have been many distinguished military officers who have attended this great school, including Grant, Lee, Patton, MacArthur, Bradley, Pershing, Eisenhower, and Schwarzkopf. It has long been recognized as one of the country's leading academic colleges, especially in the engineering fields.

Most students who enter West Point are recommended by members of Congress. This recommendation is not as difficult to receive as it might first seem. A written request to your congressional representative detailing your background and desire may be enough to get you an appointment or at least an interview at West Point. The congressmembers often do not personally know the applicants they recommend.

Active-duty soldiers can compete for class seats and often enter West Point through the US Military Academy Preparatory School. This school is designed to prepare enlisted soldiers academically and physically for the tough programs at West Point. The Preparatory School has an outstanding program of instruction, with 95 percent of its students going on to graduate from West Point. This is definitely a good career move for anyone with the desire to excel and complete a superior academic program. There are no previous college requirements except strong ACT and SAT scores, which can usually be met through the Preparatory School's intense preparation process. You can have an application sent directly to you by writing to Commandant, USMAPS, MAPSADM, Fort Monmouth, NJ 07703-5000.

OCS

Officer Candidate School is an excellent commissioning source for quality enlisted soldiers. It is a tough course with high standards that will test your limits of endurance, both mentally and physically.

To be accepted, you must have a four-year degree from an accredited college or university, US citizenship, and a GT score of at least 110. A security clearance of at least "secret" is required of all commissioned officers. You must meet height and weight standards and be able to pass the Army Physical Fitness Test (APFT). Applicants must score a 90 or better on the Officer Selection Battery (OSB) Test and be of good moral character. Minor violations of the law, including UCMJ action, can be waivered. If you need a waiver, see the sample copy in Chapter 7. The official study guide for the OSB test is DA Pamphlet 611-282.

The regulation governing Officer Candidate School eligibility criteria and application processing is AR 351-5. The selection process for OCS is highly competitive, but attending the school is well worth the effort required. Every successful graduate is commissioned a second lieutenant and obligated to three years of active duty following graduation. You wear the OCS insignia while a candidate and are paid as an E-5 unless you hold a higher rank, in which case you are paid at the higher grade.

The course is fourteen weeks long and is broken into three phases: basic officer candidate (BOC), intermediate officer candidate (IOC), and senior officer candidate (SOC). The first phase is six weeks long, followed by two four-week phases. The course is designed to be highly stressful. This is usually achieved through intense pressure to succeed, with too many missions given. The mission load is intended to be impossible so that the cadre can observe how candidates perform under pressure.

Requirements while at OCS include filling out an Officer's Assignment Preference Statement and listing at least four branch preferences. The majority of the needs are in the combat arms branches such as the infantry or armor. Many of the newly commissioned second lieutenants get detailed to a combat arms branch for three or four years, and then go back to their parent branch in the combat service support sector. You may be "branched" an ordnance officer, for instance, and "detailed" an infantry officer for four years. What this means is that your first school as an officer would be Infantry Officer Basic, with follow-on assignments in infantry positions until you make captain. As a captain, you would be sent to the Ordnance Officer Advanced Course and placed in ordnance positions thereafter.

You can request whatever branch interests you, but keep in mind that the needs of the Army take precedence over your personal choices, although the Army does try to consider what you want whenever possible. Do not let this point deter you, as you'll find the commissioned life very challenging and rewarding regardless of the branch assignment given. If you held an enlisted rank in a particular field, the possibility of being commissioned into that branch is greater. Maybe you are a Patriot maintainer (24T) and you want to become an air defense officer. This is definitely possible, and your chances are probably good, though not guaranteed. See sample checklist and contract on pages 101–102.

NAME: _____

SSN: _____

**OFFICER CANDIDATE SCHOOL
APPLICATION CHECKLIST**

DATE: _____

UNIT: _____

	ITEMS PROVIDED BY SOLDIER/UNIT	EXPLANATION	YES	NO	NA	REMARKS
1	OCS APPLICATION FORM	SIGNED BY COMMANDER & SOLDIER				
2	OCS APPLICATION CHECKLIST					
3	DD FORM 785 (RECORD OF DISSENROLLMENT FROM OCS)	IF SOLDIER HAS EVER ATTENDED OCS				
4	COPY OF **BIRTH CERTIFICATE** OR STATEMENT OF CITIZENSHIP	FULL NAME & DATE MUST BE LEGIBLE. BAPTISM CERTIFICATES ARE NOT ACCEPTABLE.				
5	COPY OF **SOCIAL SECURITY CARD**					
6	COPY OF **ID CARD**	EXPIRATION DATE NOT EARLIER THAN COMMISSIONING DATE				
7	ID TAGS	TWO TAGS WITH CHAIN				
8	COPY OF **DD 214** OR **220**	CERTIFIED TRUE COPY				
9	COPY OF **DA 2-1**	ENSURE GT SCORE IS **110** OR HIGHER.				
10	**OFFICIAL COLLEGE TRANSCRIPTS** (IN SEALED ENVELOPE)	MUST POSSESS **60** CREDITS TO ENROLL IN STATE OCS. MUST HAVE **90** CREDITS BY COMMISSIONING DATE (& TO APPLY TO ACCELERATED OCS)				
11	**SAT/ACT TEST SCORES**	REQUIRED ONLY IF SOLDIER DOES NOT HAVE 4 YR DEGREE. NEED SAT SCORE OF AT LEAST **850**, AND ACT OF AT LEAST **19**.				
12	SF 88/93 (REPORT OF MEDICAL EXAM)	MUST HAVE CHAPTER II COMMISSIONING PHYSICAL WITHIN 24 MONTHS OF COMMISSIONING DATE				
13	**DA FORM 5500** (BODY FAT)	IF APPLICABLE				
14	**DA FORM 873** (SECURITY STMT)	SOLDIER MUST HAVE SECRET CLEARANCE OR INTERIM BY COMMISSIONING DATE				
15	COPY OF SF 86 - EPSQ (REQUEST FOR SECURITY CLEARANCE) IF SOLDIER DOES NOT HAVE CLEARANCE	COMPLETED VALIDATION FORM & DISK MUST BE SUBMITTED TO STATE SECURITY OFFICER.				
16	COPY OF **DA FORM 705** (PT CARD)	SOLDIER MUST HAVE PASSED AN APFT WITHIN 12 MONTHS PRIOR TO START DATE TO APPLY				
17	COPY OF **CLOTHING RECORDS**					
18	REQUEST FOR **AGE WAIVER** (IF APPLICABLE: 30-39)	AGE WAIVER REQUIRED IF SOLDIER WILL BE OVER 30 AND UNDER 40 AS OF COMMISSIONING DATE				
19	REQUEST FOR PRIOR **CIVIL/MILITARY CONVICTIONS WAVIER** (IF APPLICABLE)	INCLUDE COURT DOCUMENTS WITH DISPOSITION OF OFFENSE, NGB FORM 62, AND MEMO FROM SOLDIER CONCERNING THE OFFENSE				
20	REQUEST FOR **MEDICAL WAVIER** (IF APPLICABLE)					
21	PROOF OF **ATRRS** DATA INPUT					
	ITEMS ADDED BY RTI					
22	AUTOBIOGRAPHY WITH PHOTOGRAPH	DONE BY SOLDIER DURING PHASE 0				
23	DA FORM 705 (PT CARD)	APFT GIVEN BY RTI DURING PH 0 (WITHIN 60 DAYS PH I)				
24	DA FORM 5500 (BODY FAT)	DONE BY RTI WITHIN 60 DAYS OF PH I				
25	ATTACHMENT ORDERS TO RTI					
26	PROMOTION ORDERS TO E6					
27	ANNUAL TRAINING ORDERS FOR PH I					

Officer Candidate School Application Checklist

ARMY OFFICER CANDIDATE CONTRACT AND SERVICE AGREEMENT

For use of this form, see AR 350-51; the proponent agency is ODCSPER.

NAME *(Last, first, MI)*	SOCIAL SECURITY NUMBER
CURRENT DUTY ASSIGNMENT	DATE OF BIRTH

EXPLANATION TO APPLICANT

An extended lead time is required to process applications for Officer Candidate School. A limited number of applicants may be selected for each class; therefore, the number of dropouts must be minimized. Accordingly, consider carefully the conditions stated below. You must understand and accept these conditions to apply.

1. If I will have insufficient service remaining in my current term of service as a member of the Regular Army at time of enrollment in OCS, I agree to extend my enlistment UP AR 601-280 for a sufficient period of time to complete OCS training.

2. If a member of a Reserve Component on active duty, I agree to remain on active duty in my present status for a sufficient period of time to permit completion of OCS training.

3. I agree to waive my enlistment commitment effective the date I accept designation as an officer candidate by Headquarters, Department of the Army *(if so designated)*. I fully understand that in the event I subsequently withdraw my application or fail to satisfactorily complete OCS training, I will not be granted my enlistment option and will be required to serve the remainder of my enlistment.

4. I agree that, if enrolled in OCS training, I will not withdraw from the training *(except as provided for in paragraph 5-11c, AR 350-51)* until I have completed at least 4 weeks of training.

5. I further agree that, upon graduation from OCS, I will accept appointment as a commissioned officer in any branch of the USAR, if tendered, and will serve for a minimum of 3 years in a commissioned status on active duty. I understand and agree that any part of my total military service obligation *(6 years for persons entering military service on or before 31 May 1984, 8 years for persons entering military service on or after 1 June 1984)* which remains at the time of appointment will be carried over for fullfillment in my commissioned status.

SIGNATURE OF APPLICANT	DATE

DA FORM 4322, JUN 2001 EDITION OF OCT 84 IS OBSOLETE. USAPPC V1.00

Army Officer Candidate Contract and Service Agreement

College Requirements and OCS

There is another issue that you should think about before you make the move to Officer Candidate School. It takes a minimum of 60 semester hours of college (with waiver) to qualify for a slot at OCS, but the minimum standard of education expected of all commissioned officers (not warrants) is a bachelor's degree. You have to have at least this level of education to compete for captain. The captain promotion board normally meets at about your third year of commissioned service. This means that you will have a little less than three years to go from 60 semester hours of college to a complete four-year degree. OCS is very competitive and most boards will not consider OCS candidates that do not already have a four-year degree on submittal. Needs are constantly changing and this may change again too.

Realistically, most of the credits for soldiers competing for OCS come from having their military experience evaluated and taking a couple of college courses and maybe one or two general CLEP tests. This may open the door for you to get into OCS, but it's a long way from an actual degree, in which you must meet specific degree requirements. You need a strategy for successful degree completion in a relatively short period of time. Your first strategy should be to finish the degree requirements before your course date. If that's not possible, plan your strategy around the OCS course and the follow-on course itself.

Chapter 6 explained how to use the ACE recommendations to further your degree goals. But what if you know up front that you are going to attend a particular school such as OCS and your branch officer basic course? These schools are worth considerable college equivalent credit and could propel you into a degree-completion program much faster than your previous enlisted courses. This is because they teach skills required of people with greater responsibility and are therefore worth more college equivalent credit.

So if you know up front which course you will be attending, then you can plan a degree-completion program accordingly. You will probably already have a designated branch of assignment prior to your OCS course start date. Even if you do not, you can still use this plan in reverse if the Army surprises you at the last minute with an unexpected officer branch assignment.

An infrequent opportunity does exist for some newly commissioned officers to pursue a degree-completion program. This program allows the lieutenant to attend a college or university full-time to complete degree requirements. Only a few officers each year are chosen to complete their degrees in this way. This must be requested through your parent commissioning branch. Those selected would normally be expected to have their degrees completed within one year. The drawback to this is that when competing for promotion to captain you will have fewer officer evaluation reports on file as compared with other officers.

What follows is a possible chain of events following that wonderful OCS selection day. SGT Branson submitted an OCS packet through the command channels and selected the Ordnance Corps as his number-one choice for officer branch assignment. He is a mechanic (63B) and wants to remain in the maintenance field as an officer. The Army agrees with his logic and has slots available for ordnance lieutenants, so he is granted his number-one branch request.

SGT Branson's packet is reviewed by the OCS review board six months later, and he is selected and given an OCS class slot that is eight months away. He now has eight months to complete as many semester hours as he can before his class date. This is a good move on SGT Branson's part, because the expectations of top performance among officers are very high. Good report cards carry a lot of weight, and even one bad officer evaluation will ruin an officer's career. Those first few years as an officer are critical to your long-term success, and degree-completion goals may limit your ability to spend as much time as your peers do in those first jobs as platoon leaders or shop officers, for example.

There are some things weighing in SGT Branson's favor. For instance, the learning curve among prior enlisted officers is probably much shorter than that for newly commissioned officers with no prior service. You will know a lot of things about the service that they don't know. But much of what you did in the past as an enlisted soldier or NCO won't correspond to your duties as a new officer—NCOs and officers have different roles and responsibilities.

Another important consideration is that many of your new peers have both prior enlisted experience and a college degree. Many ROTC and West Point officers started their careers as enlisted soldiers. The difference is that they entered into full-time degree programs and completed their degrees before reentering the service.

Here is a look at SGT Branson's enlisted military experience that can be used for college credit. Colleges will not allow duplicate credit toward a degree program.

Source of Credit	Equivalently Named Civilian Experience	Semester Hour Value
Basic Training	(1SH) Marksmanship Training, (1SH) First Aid, (1SH) Outdoor Skills, (1SH) Physical Training	4
AIT	(9SH) Automotive, Diesel, or Truck Mechanics	9
Airborne Training	(1SH) Skydiving	1
PLDC	(1SH) Supervision, (2SH) Military Science	3
BNCOC	(1SH) Personnel Supervision	1
Logistic C/Course	(4SH) Logistics Management (upper division)	4
	Total:	22

Following are ACE guide recommendations for SGT Branson's projected officer-related training:

Source of Credit	Equivalently Named Civilian Experience	Semester Hour Value
Officer Candidate School	(3SH) Principles of Management	10
	(3SH) Personnel Management	
	(3SH) Physical Education, (1SH) Map Reading	
Ordnance	(1SH) Communication Skills	15
Maintenance	(2SH) Automotive/Heavy Equipment Fundamentals	
Management Officer	(3SH) Principles of Supervision (upper division)	
Basic Course	(3SH) Vehicle Maintenance Management (UD)	
	(2SH) Fundamentals of Instruction (UD)	
	(4SH) Logistics (upper division)	
	Total:	25

SGT Branson will have to make sure that this credit is not duplicated by his previous military experience. He should meet face-to-face with a college counselor or dean and be involved in the process, or some of it might be considered duplicate. This is definitely a battle worth waging. SGT Branson can plan on earning up to 47 hours of equivalent college credit just from military-affiliated experience. This is worth about one and a half years of college. SGT Branson needs to select a degree program that best fits his credits. He doesn't have much time to finish his degree, so he's going to have to work fast and hard.

SGT Branson has eight months—only three semesters—before his OCS course starts. He has to have already taken at least two college courses, because he couldn't have had his military experience evaluated onto a transcript otherwise. Let's assume that SGT Branson has taken only those two courses so far. The minimum residency requirements for his degree are 30 semester hours of credit. That means he has to take at least eight more classes with this college to have a degree conferred to him. That does not mean that he has to finish the degree now; it just means that he has to satisfy all of the minimum constraints before leaving the area.

This is an important concept, because SGT Branson will leave this installation and probably not come back after his Officer Basic Course. He can finish similar classes at another college or university and transfer the credit back to this college to meet the remaining degree constraints. SGT Branson must make sure his current college understands his goals and advises him properly on how to achieve them. Refer to his degree program to see how he makes it fit these objectives.

Model Curriculum
Basic Skills/Liberal Arts Component

English Composition I
English Composition II
Mathematics
Natural Science
Natural Science
Social Science
Behavioral Science
History/Political Science
History/Political Science
Humanities
Humanities
Religion
Religion
Literature/Language/Speech
Philosophy
Philosophy
Free elective
Free elective
Free elective
Free elective

Management Component

Principles of Accounting I
Principles of Accounting II
Managerial Accounting
Principles of Macroeconomics
Principles of Microeconomics
Principles of Finance
Quantitative Methods
Business Statistics
Business Law
Principles of Management
Personnel Management
Managerial Communications
Management Policies and Strategies
Organizational Behavior
Free elective
Free elective
Free elective
Free elective
Free elective
Free elective

Strategy for Completion
Basic Skills/Liberal Arts Component Strategy

Took class with college/weak subject area
Took class with college/weak subject area
CLEP College Algebra/strong area
CLEP General Biology/requires review
Take class with college
CLEP Introductory Sociology/some review
Take class with college
CLEP American History 1865–Present
*Take American Foreign Policy/HI 353/UD
CLEP general exam/needs lots of review
Covered under general CLEP
*Take Paul's Missionary Journeys/REL 301/UD
*Take New Age Theory/REL 454/UD
CLEP American Literature/strong area
*Take Social Psychology/PS301/UD
*Take Special Topics/PS429/UD
Military experience/LD
Military experience/LD
Military experience/LD
Military experience/LD

Management Component Strategy

Take class with college
Take class with college
Take class with college
CLEP Introductory Macroeconomics/easy
CLEP Introductory Microeconomics/easy
Take class with college
Take class with college
Take class with college
Take class with college
Principles of Management credit from OCS
Personnel Management credit from OCS
Take class with college
Take class with college
Take class with college
Logistics Management credit/UD
Principles of Supervision credit/UD
Vehicle Maintenance Management/UD
Fundamentals of Instruction/UD
Logistics/UD
Physical Education/military experience

---

* These classes will fulfill two degree requirements: upper-division and subject-matter coverage.

Notice the equivalents that are shown in bold print: SGT Branson has an extra 11 credit hours of military experience. This is not bad, since there are still several constraints that have been met, especially in the area of upper-division credit. All of the Management Component electives except one are upper-division credit. Combine those with the five dual-credit classes from the Basic Skills curriculum, and he has 31 semester hours of projected upper-division credit. That factor alone gives SGT Branson plenty of liberty to finish the degree.

What about those unmatched credits? Is there anything at all he can do to improve this? The answer depends on the college. It is possible to request a waiver to the degree program and substitute other classes into the program structure. In SGT Branson's case, he should probably ask for an interview with the dean of admissions to explain his needs thoroughly. The ideal solution would be for the dean to give him a waiver so that the upper-division equivalent military credit could be used on a one-for-one basis to replace other required degree courses.

Assume for a minute that the dean is sympathetic to SGT Branson's request and grants waivers to allow four of the upper-division credits to replace the following required courses: Organizational Behavior, Management Policies and Strategies, Managerial Accounting, and Business Law. This would then make room for all of the other credit to be used as open electives. This would still leave SGT Branson 1 semester hour short in open elective credit. This 1 credit hour could be waived by asking the college to change its acceptance of transfer test credit hours from the normal 30 to 31. More than likely it would do so.

SGT Branson should now take three college classes per semester until he leaves for his OCS course. It would probably be best for him to take the classes that provide duplicate credit first, as these are the ones that will ensure the smoothest transfer of future courses from other colleges. In other words, instead of telling the college what he intends to do in the future, he will have demonstrated the method in actuality. Not many college students mix these two constraints. Most pick the introductory courses because those tend to be the ones everyone else is taking and the underlying theory is that they will be easier because they are introductory.

What if the college is against any of these proposals? There are alternatives. For example, SGT Branson could enroll in a college that grants only external degrees and try to get a stronger commitment from one of them. Colleges of this type often do not teach classes themselves, but only evaluate credit from other sources. The other sources can be anything from traditional classes taught at an accredited institution to military experience and equivalency exams. SGT Branson's success would probably depend on just how well he is able to match his background with their degree programs. There is no residency requirement at most of these institutions, because they charge for the evaluations that lead to degrees. The evaluations can be expensive, but not as costly as a traditional degree program.

This might be a good idea for SGT Branson, because it wouldn't matter where he is assigned. He will probably always have access to college classes that could qualify for equivalent credit. He will be safe as long as the institution is fully accredited to grant four-year degrees. This is still not going to be an easy task to complete in only eight months. He will have to give up a lot of free time to make it work. This would be an ideal time for him to take plenty of leave. He won't be able to take any time off at OCS, so he might as well take some now and eliminate some of the testing requirements and other college-related work.

GOARMY.COM GREEN-TO-GOLD PROGRAM ACCESS

The Green-to-Gold program for enlisted soldiers has become much easier to access and learn about thanks to the GoArmy.com portal. Soldiers can find out about all the current prerequisites for getting into the program and download forms and information to make packet completion much easier than in times past. This is an excellent resource for any soldier contemplating a degree-completion goal that includes additional opportunities to become a commissioned officer. The website can be found at www.goarmy.com/rotc/enlisted_soldiers.html.

PART IV

Demonstrated Techniques for Promotion and College

9

Sergeant Smith Gets Promoted

This chapter will use the example of SGT Smith to demonstrate many of the ideas suggested in this book regarding promotion. SGT Smith can be described as average in that he's a solid soldier who wishes to get promoted in a timely manner. His records to date are typical of what can be found in any Army unit for average NCOs. SGT Smith has done all the customary activities to allow him to progress to this point, but there's much more he can do.

Undoubtedly thousands of soldiers sincerely feel that they have done everything in their power to improve their promotion packets. Often they are a frustrated lot, waiting sometimes years longer than many of their peers for the promotion points to drop low enough to push them to the next rank. If you ask many of them, they believe they've done all that is possible to improve their chances for promotion. To suggest that they could drastically increase their current points to allow them to be promoted within six months might bring smirks of disbelief.

A CAREER PROGRESSION INTERVIEW WITH THE COMMANDER
Following is a career progression interview between SGT Smith and his unit commander, CPT Rusk. Note how quickly hidden promotion points are discovered.

SGT Smith: Sir, I just can't get promoted in this field. The promotion points for the 31R Communications MOS haven't dropped all year. I've already got twelve years in the Army, and I have to get promoted soon or I'll get forced out.

CPT Rusk: Well, SGT Smith, I sympathize with your predicament, but I'm not sure where you're getting that information. The promotion points for 31R SSGs have dropped several times this year. How many points do you have in your record?

SGT Smith: I have 585 points in my record, sir, and I've done everything I know to get additional promotion points. I should have been promoted a long time ago.

CPT Rusk: SGT Smith, are you maxed out on awards?

SGT Smith: Almost sir, I'm only short 10 points.

CPT Rusk: How about weapons qualification?

SGT Smith: I qualified sharpshooter with 30 hits at the M16 range last year and haven't had a chance to requalify since then.

CPT Rusk: How did you do on your last PT test?

SGT Smith: I had an overall PT score of 259—well above the company average, sir.

CPT Rusk: That's a decent score, but it's only worth 64 promotion points. That leaves 36 points available for that category. Your weapons qualification is worth 56 points, which leaves 44 points available for marksmanship qualification. How much did you earn for deployment experience?

SGT Smith: I maxed out my deployment experience category with 60 points earned toward my promotion.

CPT Rusk: That is great. Your deployment experience will help you get promoted to SSG and many more ranks to come. So, SGT Smith, how many points do you have in military education?

SGT Smith: Sir, I have 211 points in military education. I've already been to PLDC, BNCOC, NBC School, and the Combat Lifesaver Course, and I've done several correspondence courses.

CPT Rusk: You've done a lot of work on your military education, but there are still 69 points to be had in that area. How are you doing in civilian education?

SGT Smith: I need more work in that category. It's so hard to go to college anymore. I've managed to get 39 points since I came on active duty.

CPT Rusk: That still leaves 61 points available. All together you have 215 points missing from your promotion packet. Many of those points could be made up fairly easily if you make a concerted effort, say for the next ninety days, to improve your overall promotion potential. Are you willing to put in some extra effort to get promoted?

SGT Smith: Yes, sir, I want to get promoted. I never really sat down and looked at each section of my promotion packet like we just did. It's a real eye-opener to see areas of improvement that I've just kind of taken for granted.

CPT Rusk: Well, this is the first step. I've analyzed each of the MOSs in the company and discovered that every one of my soldiers could get promoted with enough work. Your MOS is a tough one, because even though it has come down seven times in the past year, those drops haven't amounted to a lot. Five times your MOS dropped to 751, once to 745, and once to 762. If we want to get you promoted in a timely manner, we'll have to look at getting your points to around 762. Maybe you won't have to max your PT test or civilian education. If we can improve each of these areas that should be enough to get you promoted quickly.

SGT Smith: Well, sir, I appreciate your concern, and I'm willing to do whatever it takes to get past this tough promotion.

CPT Rusk: One good thing about this work is that it will also benefit you further along in your career. Improving these individual areas will make you more competitive for senior NCO or warrant officer promotions. We can start today by getting you the maximum in awards. Go see SSG Bates at the motor pool and have him start the paperwork on getting you a Driver Badge. That will take care of those additional 10 points you need in awards.

This sample interview represents a very realistic scenario. SGT Smith's promotion problems may be more difficult than most soldiers will encounter because he's in an overstrength MOS with fewer chances for promotion. The remainder of this chapter will trace SGT Smith's progression in each of the six promotion point areas, with a brief look at one method for obtaining college credit quickly.

CPT Rusk had SGT Smith look at the composite of promotion points available to him, as follows:

SSG PROMOTION POINTS AVAILABLE

Section Title	Possible Points
Awards & Decorations	165
Military Training:	255
Marksmanship	(100)
Physical Readiness	(100)
Deployment Experience	(60)
Military Education	280
Civilian Education	100

Total:	800

Now that SGT Smith has decided to raise his promotion points to 762, he makes a comparison for himself so that he can develop a plan to get promoted within a few months:

SGT Smith's Prior Points for Promotion		SGT Smith's Promotion Goal	
Awards & Decorations	155	Awards & Decorations	165
Military Training:		Military Training:	
Marksmanship	56	Marksmanship	92
Physical Readiness	64	Physical Readiness	75
Deployment Experience	60	Deployment Experience	60
Military Education	211	Military Education	280
Civilian Education	39	Civilian Education	90
Total:	585	Total:	762

DUTY PERFORMANCE AND BOARD POINTS

Former semicentralized promotions contained points-driven sections for duty performance and attendance at local boards. The new program still contains these two components but now relies on the recommendation of the unit commander, coupled with the validation for promotion by a board convened locally. There are no points associated with this recommendation or the subsequent validation from the E-5 or E-6 board. It is simply a Go/No Go validation of the commander's recommended soldier for these two important levels of promotion.

PHYSICAL TRAINING IMPROVEMENT

SGT Smith takes a hard look at his promotion point potential in physical training (PT). He scored 259 points on his last record APFT and was twenty-five years old when he took the test.

SGT SMITH'S PT TEST DATA

PT Performance	Score
65 push-ups	89
67 sit-ups	83
14:12 run time	87
Total:	259

SGT Smith realizes he can improve his PT score with just a little more effort. The following table shows the breakdown of promotion points per score.

PROMOTION POINTS FOR PHYSICAL FITNESS
BASED ON APFT RECORD (FOR SSG)

SCORE = POINTS	SCORE = POINTS	SCORE = POINTS	SCORE = POINTS
300 = 100	270 = 75	240 = 45	210 = 28
299 = 99	269 = 74	239 = 44	209 = 28
298 = 99	268 = 73	238 = 43	208 = 27
297 = 98	267 = 72	237 = 42	207 = 27
296 = 98	266 = 71	236 = 41	206 = 26
295 = 97	265 = 70	235 = 41	205 = 26
294 = 97	264 = 69	234 = 40	204 = 25
293 = 96	263 = 68	233 = 40	203 = 25
292 = 96	262 = 67	232 = 39	202 = 24
291 = 95	261 = 66	231 = 39	201 = 24
290 = 95	260 = 65	230 = 38	200 = 23
289 = 94	259 = 64	229 = 38	199 = 23
288 = 93	258 = 63	228 = 37	198 = 22
287 = 92	257 = 62	227 = 37	197 = 22
286 = 91	256 = 61	226 = 36	196 = 21
285 = 90	255 = 60	225 = 36	195 = 21
284 = 89	254 = 59	224 = 35	194 = 20
283 = 88	253 = 58	223 = 35	193 = 20
282 = 87	252 = 57	222 = 34	192 = 19
281 = 86	251 = 56	221 = 34	191 = 19
280 = 85	250 = 55	220 = 33	190 = 18
279 = 84	249 = 54	219 = 33	189 = 18
278 = 83	248 = 53	218 = 32	188 = 17
277 = 82	247 = 52	217 = 32	187 = 17
276 = 81	246 = 51	216 = 31	186 = 16
275 = 80	245 = 50	215 = 31	185 = 16
274 = 79	244 = 49	214 = 30	184 = 16
273 = 78	243 = 48	213 = 30	183 = 15
272 = 77	242 = 47	212 = 29	182 = 15
271 = 76	241 = 46	211 = 29	181 = 15
			180 = 15

SGT Smith is amazed to realize that with just two more push-ups, two more sit-ups, and a 47-second decrease in his run time, he can earn 11 more PT points and 11 more promotion points.

SGT SMITH'S DESIRED PT TEST SCORES

PT Performance	Score	Improvement Required
67 push-ups	91	2 more push-ups
69 sit-ups	85	2 more sit-ups
13:30 run time	94	47-second decrease on run time
Total:	270	= 75 Point Promotion Value

SGT Smith realizes that a program of improvement can help him reach his goal by the next unit PT test. Most soldiers have access to free gyms and qualified attendants who can assist them in building individualized physical-training improvement programs. SGT Smith realizes that he will have more fun and be more likely to stick with an improvement program with the help of an athletic friend, so he calls his old friend SGT Studly to motivate him as an exercise buddy.

MARKSMANSHIP IMPROVEMENT

Marksmanship is the other portion of SGT Smith's military training portion in need of improvement. He currently holds a weapons qualification of sharp-shooter. Promotion points for marksmanship are as follows:

PROMOTION POINTS FOR MARKSMANSHIP
BASED ON FIRING RECORD FOR SSG

DA Form 3695 (M16)	DA Form 88 (Pistol)	MP Firearm Qualification Course
40 = 100	30 = 100	50 = 100
39 = 98	29 = 98	49 = 96
38 = 96	28 = 96	48 = 92
37 = 94	27 = 88	47 = 88
36 = 92	26 = 80	46 = 82
35 = 86	25 = 74	45 = 78
34 = 80	24 = 68	44 = 72
33 = 74	23 = 60	43 = 68
32 = 68	22 = 52	42 = 62
31 = 62	21 = 48	41 = 58
30 = 56	20 = 44	40 = 52
29 = 52	19 = 40	39 = 48
28 = 48	18 = 36	38 = 42
27 = 44	17 = 32	37 = 38
26 = 40	16 = 28	36 = 32
25 = 36		35 = 28
24 = 32		
23 = 28		

SGT Smith quickly sees that differences in weapons qualifications can have a major impact on promotion potential and decides that he should not wait until the next scheduled unit range to improve his qualification score. SGT Smith has lunch with SPC Bond and arranges to spend Saturday afternoon with him acquiring more marksmanship skills. Most units have several top-notch soldiers who are willing to spend additional training time helping out fellow soldiers. Many soldiers compete professionally and can provide excellent advice and training. You can also ask your unit commander to assign you a different personal weapon from the unit arms room. You might be a crack shot with an M-16 rifle but can't hit the side of a barn with an M-9 pistol. It may be worth several promotion points to ask.

AWARDS IMPROVEMENT

The awards and decorations section of the promotion packet is worth 165 promotion points (for SSG). Awards usually come with time in service. As soldiers PCS from station to station, they tend to accumulate awards.

SGT Smith has been in the unit for more than a year and has a safe driving record. Therefore, he contacts the motor pool to start the paperwork for a Driver Badge, as CPT Rusk suggested. Soon he will have the maximum 165 points in the awards area.

MILITARY EDUCATION IMPROVEMENT

SGT Smith has been struggling in the area of military education. He has only 211 points out of a possible 280. This large gap is not going to get any smaller until he makes the time to improve his score. Success here generally hinges on completing what most soldiers have already started in the form of correspondence courses. SGT Smith starts by digging through his wall locker and finding several courses that he began and never finished. He uses his calendar to partition hours needed to complete the courses he already has, and he investigates other courses that can earn him the most points for time invested.

There are smart ways to order correspondence courses that help guarantee soldier participation and success. There are many courses to choose from but not all correspondence courses carry the same weight in promotion point value. NCOES courses are a very important part of the Military Education section but only a few of the courses carry the promotion weight of a good correspondence course.

A good correspondence course can provide an excellent skill-learning platform as well as provide excellent promotion point potential for aspiring SGTs and SSGs. An added benefit of some correspondence course programs is that they can provide you with college equivalent credit as well. Logistics Management is one example of a good course for earning military credit as well as civilian credit. It is recognized in the ACE guide and can be added to your transcript if the college you attend accepts it for credit.

Army Correspondence Course Enrollment Application

For use of this form, see DA PAM 350-59; The proponent agency is TRADOC.

DATE *(YYYYMMDD)*

DATA REQUIRED BY THE PRIVACY ACT

*Submit one copy. See instructions on Back Page. Fill in All Blocks (Except **Shaded Blocks** which are for school use).*

1. Student SSN

2. Primary MOS/Duty MOS

3. CIV-SERIES

4. AOC   Duty Position

5. ASI/SQI

6. Branch

7. DSN (Telephone)

COMM (Telephone)

8. Group Number

9. Rank/Civ Grade

10. Component Code

11. RYE Date Month Day (Abbreviate) Year

12. School Grade

13. Enrollment Code

14. Phase

15. Course Number

16. Rep Qty

17. Unit Identification Code

18. Subcourse Exemption

19. I REQUEST ENROLLMENT IN: (Course Title, MOS if applicable or subcourses desired).
(Do not list individual subcourses if you are enrolling in a course).

NOTE: If you were previously enrolled in this course, indicate date of termination of enrollment. _____
Are you currently enrolled in the ACCP? _____ Yes _____ No

20. To: (School address, including ZIP Code).

THRU: (Unit to which assigned).

21. Title of approving official

Unit Address Line 1 Unit Designation (May not be left blank)

Unit Address Line 2 P.O. Box or Street (May not be left blank)

Unit Address Line 3 City, Post or APO/FPO

STATE or AE/AP/AA

ZIP + 4

FROM: (Mailing address to which subcourses are to be sent).

22. Last Name

First Name

Middle Initial

Student Address Line 1 Unit Designation or P.O. Box or Street (May not be left blank)

Student Address Line 2 P.O. Box or Street (If not given on Student Address, Line 1)

Student Address Line 3 City, Post or APO/FP

STATE or AE/AP/AA

ZIP + 4

DA FORM 145, OCT 2000   REPLACES EDITION OF JAN 1992, WHICH IS OBSOLETE   USAPA V1.00

Army Correspondence Course Enrollment Application

23.	ARMY SCHOOL COURSES AND CORRESPONDENCE COURSES COMPLETED	
SCHOOL	TITLES OF RESIDENT OR NONRESIDENT COURSES OR INDIVIDUAL SUBCOURSES COMPLETED	DATES

The Commander will verify the above from personnel records or soldier's individual records.

24. I have reviewed DA PAM 350-59, and understand the eligibility requirements that I must maintain to sustain my enrollment in this course. I further understand that assistance is not authorized when completing subcourse test.

Signature of Applicant _____

25. I have reviewed the course objectives and prerequisite enrollment requirements in DA PAM 350-59 and determined the applicant is eligible for enrollment in this course.

Unit Cdr or other approving officer.
Name (printed or typed) _____ Date *(YYYYMMDD)* _____

Signature _____

DA PAM 350-59 contains information pertaining to enrollment qualifications,
submission of application and courses available.

INSTRUCTIONS TO APPLICANT

Complete by legibly printing only in areas that are not shaded. The shaded areas are used for data entry. Enter only one character per block (example below).

1. Student SSN

2	4	4	3	2	0	1	6	4

9. Rank/Civ Grade

S	G	T	M	A	J

ITEM 1.   SSN: Foreign students must leave blank.

ITEM 2.   Student's PMOS (Primary MOS) and DMOS (Duty MOS). Enter numeric and alpha identifiers.

ITEM 3.   Civ-Series number (for example 1702).

ITEM 4.   AOC Area of Concentration or Duty Position. Submit information required to qualify for enrollment.

ITEM 9.   RANK: RA warrant officers and enlisted personnel who hold a reserve commission and are enrolling in officer career development courses must enroll in their reserve capacity.

ITEM 10. Component Code: Student categories: Enter one of the following as appropriate:

02 Active Duty Officer	09 USAR ENL	15 FGN CIV	20 CADET
03 RA/AUS ENL	10 NGUS ENL	16 USAF	31 IRR (OFF)
06 RET MILITARY	12 NDCC/ROTC/JR	17 USN	32 IRR (ENL)
07 USAR OFF/WO	13 FGN MIL	18 USCG	33 NAF (VOL)
08 NGUS OFF/WO	14 U.S. CIV	19 USMC	

ITEM 11. RYE Date (Retirement Year Ending Date): USAR and NG applicants not on active duty must enter the anniversary date of their retirement year ending day and month.

Where to mail application:
SCHOOL MAILING ADDRESS: Please check DA PAM 350-59 for appropriate address of school with whom you are seeking enrollment, e.g Academy of Health Science, The Judge Advocate General's School, Army Logistics Management College, or the Army Institute for Professional Development, etc.

REVERSE OF DA FORM 145, OCT 2000

USAPA V1.00

Army Correspondence Course Enrollment Application *continued*

SGT Smith is concerned about the amount of time all of this will take him. After all, he enjoys sports and leisure activities. He is willing to make some adjustments to meet his long-term goals, but he wants to make certain that his expectations are attainable. He decides to figure out if he can reasonably accomplish his goals in only a three-month period. Following is a possible timetable in which his military education goals will be met within three months:

Steps Toward Maxing Military Education	Time Required
Driving to Education Center	10 minutes
Reviewing *Correspondence Course Catalog* (DA Pam 351-20)	1 hour
Selecting six high-point-value selected subcourses	10 minutes
Filling out DA Form 145 for subcourses	5 minutes
Taking request form back to commander for signature	10 minutes
Sending request form to Correspondence Center in envelope provided	3 days
Review of request and processing of subcourses by Correspondence Center	3 weeks
Waiting for books to arrive by fourth-class mail	10 days
Working on books over weekend	3 days
Filling out another DA Form 145 (Figure 7) for four more subcourses	1 day
Sending completed answer sheets and new request to Correspondence Center	3 days
Grading of sheets and mailing back grades by Correspondence Center	2 weeks
Processing of subcourse request and mailing of new books by Correspondence Center	10 days
Completing books and mailing back answer sheets	10 days
Grading of sheets and mailing back of grades by Correspondence Center	2 weeks
Adding 49 points to promotion packet	1 day
Total time:	3 months

Smith is excited about the prospect of completing so much in such a short period of time. He wishes he had started working on promotion points a little earlier in his career.

CIVILIAN EDUCATION PROMOTION POINTS THROUGH TESTING

The military education problem really is not too difficult to fix because it doesn't interfere with SGT Smith's duty day very much. Most units will allow a soldier to visit the Education Center to sign up for correspondence courses without much hassle. But civilian educational credit obtained through testing (such as CLEP and DANTES) is more time-consuming, and soldiers may have difficulty getting time off from their jobs to prepare properly for this process. Taking these college credit tests, however, can be incredibly beneficial to a promotion packet—a soldier earns 1 promotion point for each credit hour.

SGT Smith realizes that he won't need to take any more traditional college classes to reach the full 100 points possible for civilian education. Instead, he decides to obtain the remaining credit through civilian testing. He has heard from SPC Kaplan that taking CLEP and DANTES tests is a great way to obtain college credit through civilian education. The Education Center has all the information necessary to aid SGT Smith in his pursuit. He also makes an appointment with a counselor at a local college to make sure the tests will fulfill the college's degree program requirements.

SGT Smith knows he will have to fit the testing into his schedule. Though he is a good soldier and well-liked by the commander, he is allowed only a few hours at the Education Center in any given month. SGT Smith anticipates this predicament and decides to ask his commander to grant him five days of leave so that he can work on building his civilian education points. The commander approves his leave request, and SGT Smith now has five working days to spend at the Education Center and his local college.

His leave begins next week, so he calls the Education Center to get all the necessary information on testing times and locations. The Education Center counselor tells SGT Smith that he can take pretests on a walk-in basis but that the real exams have to be scheduled through the Post Testing Center. SGT Smith learns that the pretests are tools that will enable him to discover how strong or weak he is in the various subject areas available for testing. On his installation, there are six testing times per week: 0830 and 1230 hours on Monday, Wednesday, and Friday. He can schedule up to two tests per period, not to exceed twelve tests per week.

SGT Smith realizes that he needs to find out this week which exams to take on Monday so as not to waste those two testing opportunities. He asks his platoon sergeant for permission to spend two hours at the Education Center to take some pretests this week. His platoon sergeant agrees to let him have two hours' time off on Wednesday afternoon.

SGT Smith goes to the Education Center at 1400 hours on Wednesday and asks the counselor for the pretests for several math tests. This is a good strategy, because math has always been SGT Smith's best subject. SGT Smith finishes four pretests in a little over an hour and then decides to try the pretests in Introduction to Business and Introduction to Law Enforcement. SGT Smith is pleasantly surprised when the counselor assures him that he has done well enough on the pretests to challenge all six exams. He then fills out the paperwork to take four of them on Monday and the other two on Wednesday morning. He informs the counselor that he'll also be in on Tuesday in civilian clothes to try some more pretests. She assures him that he'll have plenty of time to schedule any Wednesday afternoon exams should he perform well on those Tuesday pretests.

The following table shows which tests SGT Smith took and how he scored on both the pretests and the actual exams. The Education Center was able to tell

him if he passed (70+) or failed immediately following the exams, but he had
to wait about six weeks to receive the official test scores through the mail.

Test Title	Semester Hours	Pretest Score	Actual Score	Time
General Math CLEP	6	82	79	4 weeks
College Algebra CLEP	3	74	71	5 weeks
Business Math CLEP	3	90	84	4 weeks
Geometry DANTES	3	70	72	3 weeks
Intro to Business DANTES	3	80	76	3 weeks
Intro to Law Enf DANTES	3	70	72	5 weeks
Money & Banking DANTES	3	50	didn't take	—
Fundamentals of Counseling	3	80	80	4 weeks
Foundations of Education	3	30	didn't take	—
Criminal Justice	3	80	72	5 weeks
American History 1865–Pres	3	77	78	3 weeks
Introduction to Carpentry	3	40	didn't take	—
Principles of Public Speaking	3	70	68	4 weeks
Organizational Behavior	3	50	didn't take	—
American Literature	3	20	didn't take	—
Here's to Your Health	3	80	79	5 weeks
Intro to Macroeconomics	3	58	with study 71	4 weeks
Intro to Microeconomics	3	54	with study 71	4 weeks
Introductory Sociology	3	68	69	4 weeks
Introductory Business Law	3	45	didn't take	—
Basic Marketing	3	55	with study 76	5 weeks
Basic Automotive Service	3	30	didn't take	—
Introduction to Management	3	60	with study 82	4 weeks
Info Syst & Comp Appl	3	40	didn't take	—
American History to 1877	3	72	75	3 weeks
American Government	3	66	67	5 weeks
Environment & Humanity	3	60	60	5 weeks
History of West Civ I	3	40	didn't take	—
Principles of Supervision	3	80	79	4 weeks

Total passed (score 70+): 16 exams worth 51 semester hours

Smith did not do well on some of the pretests, but they still provided a
valuable service, allowing him to properly allocate his study time to maximize his areas of strength. He did not waste time taking the exams in which
he failed miserably on the corresponding pretests. SGT Smith was close to a
passing score on a few pretests and had to do some review before taking the

real test. Fortunately, he was able to take several exams without any preparation except the pretests. SGT Smith really has to push himself to solve all of his career progression problems within such a short period of time. He potentially would have to take additional days of leave to finish up his civilian education goals.

How realistic is it that a soldier be able to pass sixteen college-level examinations? It is very realistic for most people. Most soldiers have a varied enough background, are intelligent, and are relatively good test takers. There are thousands of tests available in a wide host of fields. The key is to find those tests that fit your strengths and background and take them. Most Education Centers and public libraries have DVDs and books that teach you how to be a good test taker.

Tips on Test Taking

The largest time constraint centers around tests you have to spend extra study time on. There is a "secret formula" one can use to efficiently prepare to pass even difficult exams. In our example, SGT Smith scored 58 percent on his Macroeconomics pretest. That score is actually pretty good considering that SGT Smith has never taken any economics courses. He probably gained his knowledge from books, magazine articles, television programs, word of mouth, and just good common sense. Now the goal for test-taking purposes is for him to go from the 58 percent level to about 70 to 75 percent. He doesn't need to become a subject matter expert; he only needs a little more familiarity with the subject matter. Achieving this familiarity is the "secret formula."

Familiarity is much easier to achieve than you might think. There is an axiom in economics called Pareto's Principle. Simply stated, it says that 80 percent of all profit is earned on 20 percent of all products, and 20 percent of your employees produce 80 percent of your results. This rule actually bears considerable truth in many areas of life. You can see it applied in just about everything you do. Now apply this principle to the art of study.

SGT Smith applies Pareto's Principle on a visit to the local public library, where he is looking for a good textbook on economics. First he applies the principle to the catalog search. Without a background in economics, SGT Smith is not sure who the economics experts are. He checks the subject index to see which author's name seems to reappear on economics books. Sure enough, one author's name keeps showing up. He has found his expert.

Of course, the macroeconomics expert writes much more about macroeconomics than SGT Smith has time to digest. So how does one become familiar with the 20 percent that is important to know? Well, if the author designed his textbook the way most authors do, there will be chapter summaries that can be reviewed in order to gather the important highlights. If the textbook is four hundred pages long and has twenty-five chapters, the summaries might be expected to be two to three pages long. So SGT Smith would read each of these summaries a couple of times to achieve familiarity with the subject. If there are no summaries, then a review of chapter headings, key definitions, and first and last sentences of each topic area can also be used to gain knowledge of a subject. Even a four hundred-page book can be skimmed quickly using these techniques.

The main reason that familiarity, and not necessarily expertise, is required to pass these types of exams is that they are made up of multiple-choice questions. In other words, the answer is always provided on the test. You can be sure that no matter how hard the question, one of the four or five possible answers provided is the correct one. Not only is the right answer there, but there may even be an obviously wrong answer given, which increases your odds of successfully choosing the right answer.

Most equivalency exams offer four possible answers. If you read the question and are clueless, then your probability of getting a correct answer by guessing is 25 percent. Now, what is the probability that you know absolutely nothing about the question and all four or five possible answers? Particularly if you have reviewed well, you should be able to increase your chances of choosing the correct answer by using a process of incorrect answer elimination and common sense.

How about a test of this theory? See if you can eliminate some or all of the obviously incorrect answers in the following example. Even eliminating one or two helps the odds of coming up with the correct answer.

> Which one of the following definitions best describes the meaning
> of the word *perestroika*?
>   a. An organic compound used as a paint remover and solvent.
>   b. An economic and bureaucratic restructuring.
>   c. A pot roast of beef marinated in vinegar.
>   d. Something invented, made up, or fabricated as it applies to
>   the imagination.

Now let's apply some test-taking techniques. First, try pronouncing the word silently to yourself to see if you can jog your memory. Do any of the four answers strike you as likely? How about obviously unlikely? This is where you should listen to your subconscious, or your initial gut reaction. It seldom fails.

Here is a careful look at each potential answer. Answer *a* says that this word defines a type of organic compound used to remove paint. You probably have used paint-removal products over the years. Does the word *perestroika* remind you of something on the list of ingredients for paint removers? Answer *b* states that the word deals with an economic and bureaucratic restructuring. Do you have any familiarity with any national or world events that might prompt you to believe this one? How about answer *c*? Could this be a fancy pot roast? Answer *d* is especially possible, based on the fact that there may be a trick answer. Maybe *perestroika* is a big word to describe the process of using your imagination.

You should have dismissed the fancy pot roast answer fairly quickly. Assuming that you did, your chances of getting the correct answer have improved considerably. As a matter of fact, now the odds are in your favor. You might ask how the odds could be in your favor when there is still a 66 percent chance of getting the wrong answer. That is true, but that would be measuring the wrong element of the test. You should be measuring your success by the probability of doing better than the test already allows. This calls for further explanation.

If you take a test and there are one hundred questions, it can be assumed that you will get at least twenty-five of the questions correct, even if you just randomly guess on the answer sheet. This is very much like tossing a coin to see whether it lands heads or tails. In a random toss, it might be hard to second-guess the outcome, but if all you are testing for is whether 50 percent of the time it lands tails, then that becomes much easier to predict and prove through experimentation.

Educated guessing is a totally different matter. This is more like weighting the dice. The probability of rolling a "lucky seven" is very high if the dice have been fixed to gravitate to a particular side. Even with a fixed set of dice, they will not always roll lucky sevens. But the probability is much higher, and over the length of a long game, the person with a pair of fixed dice will eventually outperform the person relying on a standard set of dice. Therefore, every incorrect answer eliminated during the testing process is similar to weighting the dice in your favor.

Closely examine answer *a* and see if it jogs your memory as an ingredient in paint remover. Maybe you don't even remember the names of those ingredients. That's the point. If *perestroika* does not jog your memory as it pertains to paint removers, then it probably is not a paint-removing ingredient. See if the following terms produce a different result: methyl acetate, methanol, methylene chloride, mineral spirits, ethanol, and methanol. Do these words sound more like what you would expect? Of course they do, since they are common ingredients in paint removers.

In truth, many people fail these exams because they simply freeze and give up. Remember that most of the clues are found by carefully examining the potential answers. The tests are based on the competence and test results of average, or C, students. Good reasoning is an important component toward success and can often overcome a lack of full knowledge of a subject area.

Even math tests can be beat by applying sound reasoning. One constraint with math tests is that time is usually against you. So how do you increase your test score on a math test when most people will not finish all of the problems? Again, strategy is the key to success. Imagine a CLEP General Math test with ninety problems and only ninety minutes given for completion. That translates to one minute per problem. There are lots of problems that you could solve if you had five minutes. There are also several problems that can be answered in a few seconds. The first strategy is to go through the entire test, answering everything you can quickly. Do not spend any time on a tough problem.

Many math questions can be answered through quick problem-solving techniques. Let me give you a few examples. What is 96 + 109 + 37? Your answer should have been about 240, because you should round the component numbers to 100 + 100 + 40 = 240. Don't worry about small numbers. Round up or down as fast as you can think, and worry about leftovers later. Fractions work the same way: $1/2 + 3/4 + 7/16 + 4^1/8 = 6$. Why? Because $1/2 + 1/2 + 4 + 1 = 6$. And again a little more specific: $7/16$ is almost $1/2$, $3/4$ plus $1/8$ is almost a whole, and 4 and $1/2$ are obvious. Obviously, this technique may help you on only a few problems. It's only meant to demonstrate that test-taking techniques *are* available. Check with your local Education Center or post library and other public libraries for videos and other valuable aids to make you a good test taker. Make use of these tools, and grow yourself into a strong career-progression-minded soldier.

SERGEANT SMITH'S PROGRESS

SGT Smith has good reason to be pleased with his results thus far. He was able to earn 51 promotion points from 51 semester hours of credit through equivalency-test taking (i.e. 1 promotion point for each credit hour earned). These 51 points will help him get closer to maximizing his civilian education points. Look at the table that follows, and compare his previous promotion point strategy with his recent successes.

SGT Smith's Prior Points for E-6 Promotion		SGT Smith's Current Point Standing	
Awards & Decorations	155	Awards & Decorations	165
Military Training:		Military Training:	
Marksmanship	56	Marksmanship	92
Physical Readiness	64	Physical Readiness	75
Deployment Experience	60	Deployment Experience	60
Military Education	211	Military Education	280
Civilian Education	39	Civilian Education	90
Total:	565	Total:	762

This example should spur many soldiers to take a good look at their promotion potential. With these good results, SGT Smith likely soon will be SSG Smith.

10

Sergeant Jones Goes to College

SGT Jones has a background that is relatively common for an Army sergeant. Just like SGT Branson of Chapter 8, he is a mechanic (63B). He has four years of active-duty service, has been to Airborne Training, PLDC, and BNCOC, and has completed the Logistics Management correspondence course. SGT Jones is on the promotion standing list for staff sergeant. He has a GT score of 104 and has never taken a college course or any college-level equivalency exams. His first sergeant has advised him to look into obtaining at least an associate's degree in order to improve his potential for promotion to E-6 and beyond.

USING AN AARTS TRANSCRIPT EFFECTIVELY

SGT Jones visits his local Education Center and fills out an AARTS transcript request form. He receives the following "unofficial" evaluation of his military experience.

Source of Credit	Equivalently Named Civilian Experience	Semester Hour Value
Basic Training	(1SH) Marksmanship Training, (1SH) First Aid, (1SH) Outdoor Skills, (1SH) Physical Training	4
AIT	(9SH) Automotive, Diesel, or Truck Mechanics	9
Airborne Training	(1SH) Skydiving	1
PLDC	(1SH) Supervision, (2SH) Military Science	3
BNCOC	(1SH) Personnel Supervision	1
Logistic C/Course	(4SH) Logistics Management (upper division)	4
	Total:	22

Keep in mind that this is an unofficial transcript and does not have any inherent value, except that it gives colleges an easy assessment tool for granting equivalent college transcript credit. No college or university, with the exception of those bound by a SOCAD agreement, has to accept this evaluation. The information found on an AARTS transcript comes from the ACE guide.

According to the AARTS recommendation, 22 semester hours of credit could be granted by SGT Jones's prospective college. The problem is that the credit recognized may not exactly fit the degree requirements. This is a problem that many soldiers encounter when trying to get their military experience evaluated.

SERGEANT JONES VISITS HIS COLLEGE ADVISOR

SGT Jones makes an appointment to visit one of the reputable colleges located near the Army installation. After taking a campus tour and speaking with a college advisor, SGT Jones decides to pursue a four-year, 120-semester-hour management curriculum toward a Bachelor of Arts degree. Following are the requirements necessary to complete the degree at the college:

BACHELOR OF ARTS DEGREE WITH A MAJOR IN MANAGEMENT

Basic Skills/Liberal Arts Component	Semester Hours	Management Component	Semester Hours
English Composition I	3	Principles of Accounting I	3
English Composition II	3	Principles of Accounting II	3
Mathematics	3	Managerial Accounting	3
Natural Science	6	Principles of Macroeconomics	3
Social Science	3	Principles of Microeconomics	3
Behavioral Science	3	Principles of Finance	3
History/Political Science	6	Quantitative Methods	3
Humanities	6	Business Statistics	3
Religion	6	Business Law	3
Literature/Language/Speech	3	Principles of Management	3
Philosophy	6	Personnel Management	3
Free electives (classes you choose)	12	Managerial Communications	3
Total:	60	Managerial Policies and Strategies	3
		Organizational Behavior	3
		Free electives (classes you choose)	18
		Total:	60

THE COLLEGE EVALUATES SERGEANT JONES'S CREDIT

During SGT Jones's initial interview at the college, the advisor agrees to grant 12 semester hours of credit on a one-for-one basis between the ACE recommendation and the lower-division electives. The advisor also agrees to count the 4 semester hours of credit from the Logistics Management correspondence course toward some of the upper-division elective requirements. SGT Jones takes the prospective curriculum and the college catalog home to study how his military experience and possibly some other nontraditional credit, such as CLEP tests, might meet the degree requirements. SGT Jones examines the degree program to see if he can develop a working strategy for meeting the many requirements. The areas where SGT Jones's military experience fulfills curriculum requirements are shown in bold print.

Model Curriculum	**Strategy for Completion**
Basic Skills/Liberal Arts Component	*Basic Skills/Liberal Arts Component Strategy*
English Composition I	Take class with college/weak subject area
English Composition II	Take class with college/weak subject area
Mathematics	Take Math 101
Natural Science	CLEP General Biology/requires review
Natural Science	Take class with college
Social Science	CLEP Introductory Sociology/some review
Behavioral Science	Take class with college
History/Political Science	CLEP American History 1865–Present
History/Political Science	*Take American Foreign Policy/HI 353/UD
Humanities	CLEP general exam/needs lots of review
Humanities	Covered under general CLEP
Religion	*Take Paul's Missionary Journeys/REL 301/UD
Religion	*Take New Age Theory/REL 454/UD
Literature/Language/Speech	CLEP American Literature/strong area
Philosophy	*Take Social Psychology/PS301/UD
Philosophy	*Take Special Topics/PS429/UD
Free elective	**Military Experience/LD**
Free elective	**Military Experience/LD**
Free elective	**Military Experience/LD**
Free elective	**Military Experience/LD**
Management Component	*Management Component Strategy*
Principles of Accounting I	Take class with college
Principles of Accounting II	Take class with college
Managerial Accounting	Take class with college
Principles of Macroeconomics	CLEP Introductory Macroeconomics/easy
Principles of Microeconomics	CLEP Introductory Microeconomics/easy
Principles of Finance	Take class with college
Quantitative Methods	Take class with college
Business Statistics	Take class with college
Business Law	Take class with college

(*continued*)

Principles of Management	**XXX Logistics Management/UD**
Personnel Management	**XXX Supervision Credit/LD**
Managerial Communications	Take class with college
Management Policies and Strategies	Take class with college
Organizational Behavior	Take class with college
Free elective	**DANTES Introduction to Business
Free elective	**DANTES Introduction to Law Enforcement
Free elective	**DANTES Fundamentals of Counseling
Free elective	**DANTES Principles of Public Speaking
Free elective	**XXX DANTES Criminal Justice**
Free elective	**XXX Military Experience/LD (4 SH)**

* Requires prerequisite class or instructor approval. Will need to convince professor of ability to do well in class. Will state willingness to withdraw if necessary.
** Requires waiver of maximum equivalent test credit. Letters of recommendation from chain of command may tip decision in his favor.
UD = upper-division course; LD = lower-division course.
XXX = Unused military experience from lower division (LD) allowed by college because several upper division (UD) constraints were met by taking UD classes to satisfy LD requirements, e.g., REL 301 for Basic Skills.

The strategy SGT Jones develops has him taking twenty classes with the college, for a total of 60 semester hours. Completing the degree program without any transfer of military experience credit or nontraditional credit would require a minimum of forty classes.

In his strategy, SGT Jones plans to take five upper-division classes that will satisfy both upper- and lower-division course requirements. His college offers several choices to meet the lower-division 6-credit-hour religion requirement: Introduction to the New Testament (REL 101), Paul's Missionary Journeys (REL 301), New Age Theory (REL 454), and Introduction to Islam (REL 201). As discussed in Chapter 5, if SGT Jones chooses REL 101 and REL 201, he will satisfy the degree requirements satisfactorily, but if he chooses REL 301 and REL 454, he will satisfy two degree needs. These two courses meet the religion course requirements for 6 semester hours and also help satisfy the *minimum upper-division 39-semester-hour* requirement. He uses the same technique with two philosophy classes and one history class. SGT Jones's careful selection of classes allows for more freedom in crafting his overall degree program.

SERGEANT JONES REVISITS HIS COLLEGE ADVISOR
On a later visit to the college, SGT Jones asks his college advisor to accept the 4 semester hours of Logistics Management and the 2 semester hours in Supervision as exchange credit against the Principles of Management and the Personnel Management courses outlined in the degree program. He also asks for

the remaining 4 semester hours of military experience to be applied toward four of the upper-division elective requirements. His advisor agrees to accept this proposal contingent upon SGT Jones's successful completion of the five additional upper-division classes intended to jointly fulfill both lower-division and upper-division requirements.

SERGEANT JONES REGISTERS FOR HIS FIRST CLASS

SGT Jones decides to start with a math course, which was an easy subject for him in high school. Additionally, SGT Jones's unit will be in the field for two weeks of the semester. He reasons that math classes are good "field" classes, since problem solving will not require library work or computer access.

Especially since he will be in the field for some of the semester, SGT Jones contacts each of the two professors who will be teaching the math classes. SGT Jones does not get the feeling that Professor Leonard is willing to grant him any flexibility due to his field duty. Professor Stratford, however, apparently is accustomed to his students having outside conflicts and states that he will allow SGT Jones to do his math work ahead of time, with his assistance. SGT Jones signs up for the math class with Professor Stratford.

SGT Jones is pleasantly surprised at his first college class experience. He expected to have some trouble readjusting to school after so many years since his high school graduation. Instead, he finds that his military training, as well as his maturity and work experience, allow him to be one of the more outgoing students in the class. He finds that he is much more focused and has few problems committing to classwork. He also finds the coursework less challenging than many of the Army courses he has taken.

Once SGT Jones takes a class or two and knows some of the other students, he hears of other professors who are likely to understand his unique needs as a soldier. It is a wise strategy to choose classes and professors with as much care as possible. Some professors give a large amount of outside-class work, and some require more class presentations than others. Some give easier exams than others. Knowing these things can help students choose the classes and professors that fit most comfortably with their learning style.

SERGEANT JONES'S COLLEGE SUCCESSES

SGT Jones used his military training, experiences, and resources, such as the Education Center, as a springboard for gaining a solid civilian education. He was able to obtain the same educational credentials as other students at much lower costs. In addition, he saved considerable time. This time savings is often the critical factor for success in completing degree requirements for military soldiers.

SGT Jones did well in college. He took charge of his college experience and was thereby positively rewarded with a military career that is progressing well. He will no doubt go on to be a strong senior leader.

PART V

Special Topics

11

Overcoming Major
Career Progression Problems

There are some reading this book who are fighting to stay in the military. This chapter is written for you. Maybe you are about to reach your retention control point (RCP), or maybe you have been selected for qualitative management program (QMP) action and are about to be eliminated from the Army. Is there something you can do to stop the process? You bet there is! However, it is not going to be easy. Such cases are very time-consuming and generally require more work than officer selection programs. But they are definitely something soldiers can deal with successfully.

First, we should eliminate any confusion over QMP and RCP actions. Both of these actions are administrative in nature. They are not legal actions. Soldiers often confuse this important issue and thus put forth an attempt to have the Army rehear their cases. The truth of the matter is that the Department of the Army can force a soldier out for poor performance and there is not much, legally speaking, that one can do about it. The legal system can be a tool to leverage a soldier's way out of an administrative action, but it is still simply an argument for his or her position and not a legal right to reverse the action.

QMP
Following is a look at QMP actions and some ways to improve your chances for retention on active duty. There are really only two types, with several sub-categories. QMP actions that result from untimely promotions are not discussed here. If you read the remainder of this book, there is more than enough information contained within these pages to prevent future QMP actions against you simply because you couldn't make SGT or SSG in a "timely" fashion. Instead, we will tackle the tough QMP actions—the ones that most soldiers fail to defeat and thus face subsequent elimination from the Army.

QMP boards normally do not look at soldier records unless there are two or more unfavorable records on file in their performance records. It takes just one unfavorable record in a military file to eliminate a soldier from the Army under QMP action in cases in which the offense is considered severe. If a soldier has committed a grievous offense, there is little to do except to prepare to exit the Army.

The vast majority of QMP actions do not involve grievous offenses, however. Most involve administrative actions resulting from letters of reprimand, Article 15s, and negative NCOERs. While it is normal for soldiers to be eliminated based on two or more bad records in their file, these two bad records sometimes stem from the same event. Soldiers who have had excellent careers otherwise may find themselves exiting the Army because of one mishap.

An Example of a QMP Action

Following is a typical scenario that could easily lead to QMP action and dismissal from the service, even for a previously solid soldier. SGT Becker is an excellent soldier who is currently teaching at the NCO Academy. He is well-liked but known for his offhand jokes. One day he is less respectful than he should be and makes an inappropriate comment to a female trainee. Though SGT Becker is only joking and does not intend to offend her, she does not appreciate his "humor" and reports the incident.

The battalion commander is also not amused by the story and believes SGT Becker's conduct is unbecoming of a soldier in his unit. The commander calls the Judge Advocate General's (JAG) Office for advice on how best to handle the situation. The attorney advises the commander to handle it as an administrative case. The attorney's reasoning is sound because it's a case of "he said/she said" and is not easily prosecuted as a legal case.

The battalion commander agrees with the attorney's recommendation and directs the subordinate commander to give SGT Becker a relief-for-cause NCOER. A few days later, the battalion commander gives SGT Becker an administrative letter of reprimand for conduct unbecoming a noncommissioned officer. The letter of reprimand has the standard statement included that says, "This action is administrative in nature and is not being used as legal action against you." No real burden of proof is required for such administrative actions.

SGT Becker is relieved from his teaching post and moved to a nontraining position. In truth, the ETS clock starts ticking for SGT Becker the moment the paperwork is finished. He technically still has an ETS date several years away, but that will be insignificant after about six to eighteen months, because the adverse action will likely trigger the QMP review process. This is particularly likely when the Army is downsizing. SGT Becker will receive a DA bar to reenlistment shortly thereafter. He will then receive notice that his file is being reviewed before the next QMP board. SGT Becker can submit matters of extenuation or mitigation and anything else he considers pertinent to his case to remain on active duty.

The question as to whether SGT Becker is truly guilty of an offense worthy of ending his military career never gets thoroughly addressed. This is true for many soldiers who find themselves in similar situations. Even if SGT

Becker is guilty of the charges against him, there is some question as to whether the offense is severe enough to end ten years of service with an excellent prior record.

Steps in Addressing a QMP Action

The first order of business for SGT Becker is to remain on active duty past the proposed ETS date. If your personnel file has already been reviewed by a QMP board and you have orders designating a new ETS date, you have to work fast to extend the ETS date by seeking a thirty-day extension. Be prepared that if your chain of command is not behind you in your attempt to remain on active duty, this job becomes significantly more difficult. If there is a sense of non-commitment either way within the chain, then you will have to do a lot on your own. Essentially this means that you will have to do most of the legwork, such as typing up the paperwork. As long as the command is willing to sign the paperwork, you are still making progress. Now you need to be extended beyond your current ninety-day window. Normally this is done in thirty-day increments. Get ready—it may take several extensions to see this through.

The extension is usually simple to obtain, as it only requires a memorandum from your commander and a verbal acknowledgment from the Department of the Army. See your retention NCO and start the paperwork. It is not difficult unless your commander says no. Then you have to get another, higher-ranking commander to say yes. Obviously this gets more time-consuming as you go up the chain. Remember the open-door policy and use it to your advantage. Certainly you can't force your superiors to agree with you—this is an administrative action and not a legal one—but you should still seek all the help you can to make your case. Use past and present commanders, supervisors, and anyone else who believes in your case.

There are actually two actions that need to happen simultaneously. If you are relieved for a circumstance similar to SGT Becker's, you have a good chance of a successful appeal to the negative NCOER. Gather everything you can that even remotely pertains to your case, and go to your local Legal Assistance Office. Set up an appointment to see an attorney so that you can review your file together. The lawyer will document the case for you in a legal fashion based on Army regulations, policy, and the laws of the state. This is still an administrative case, as you will discover when the paperwork comes back ready for your signature, but this is still a good defense.

According to AR 600-20, relief for cause must be based on substantial and credible evidence. Now what is substantial and credible evidence? From an attorney's standpoint "he said/she said" cases are not at all substantial. This is not a legal battle, however. From a commander's standpoint, he or she may not care that his case would not hold up in court. The commander probably understood that from the outset, or he or she would have chosen UCMJ or judicial proceedings.

If the SGT Becker scenario had gone to court, the prosecuting attorney would try to disparage SGT Becker's character and prove that he was only caught doing what he normally does. The defense lawyer would make a case for his long-standing perfect record of military service. The point to all of this is that the same argument still needs to be made, except that it will be presented to board members acting on administrative matters instead of a judge or jury. You have to convince the Department of the Army that your case is unique and was handled poorly by the persons involved.

If you cannot make a strong argument, then prepare to exit the Army. Board members have heard "I didn't do it" before. Anticipate the board's pessimism toward your file, and prepare accordingly. If you really are innocent, there is one other option to help give your case a boost in the eyes of your chain of command. Many installations have polygraph machines that are used by the Criminal Investigation Division (CID). You cannot be forced to take a test, but you can volunteer to take one. Keep in mind that the report can be used by the chain of command regardless of whether it turns out in your favor. Also, a good machine operator can tell if you are hiding something. Favorable test results can make all the difference in the world, as they add validity to your testimony. Polygraph tests are not regarded as solid proof, but they do alleviate some doubts and can strengthen your case.

The NCOER is appealed through the Department of the Army's Enlisted Records and Evaluation Center. A strong letter from your legal assistance attorney is your best hope of making a successful appeal. Remember to take anything remotely related to the case, plus such records as your 201 file, award recommendations, letters of recommendation, PT cards, and anything positive that would help substantiate your claims.

The QMP action can be appealed in two ways. The most common appeal process is to the QMP board itself, in which case you'll have to show reason for the board to reconsider your case. You need to show that they were lacking all the facts. This is where you use all your bullets. Give them letters from your chain of command, supervisors, previous supervisors, the letter from the legal assistance lawyer, your positive results from the polygraph test, your successful NCOER appeal or pending appeal, copies of things not in your permanent file (they have an official microfiche), and anything else that makes your case stronger. The better-supported your case, the higher your chances for success.

The QMP board falls under the Office of the Deputy Chief of Staff for Personnel (DCSPER) located in the Pentagon. The board receives its guidelines from the DCSPER, and thus its decisions can be overridden by this higher office. If your chain of command is behind you, ask them to make a telephone call on your behalf. The more chain-of-command involvement, the more likely a favorable ruling. Such support does not have to come from the entire chain. Maybe only the company commander believes in you. Or maybe the first sergeant and the first-line supervisors. This may be enough. Boards are obviously apprehensive about issuing QMP reversals that are not supported by the chain of command.

The second way of addressing a QMP action is through an appeal to have the bad documents either thrown out altogether or placed in your restricted fiche. This action is done through the Department of the Army's Suitability and Evaluations Board. The guidelines for these two actions are found in AR 27-10 and AR 600-37. Review the appropriate chapters before writing your appeal, as you want to make your argument in accordance with the regulatory guidelines. If you make the wrong request, it will get disapproved for poor logic.

The Suitability and Evaluations Board normally considers two years to be the minimum time standard to approve requests for negative items to be moved from the performance fiche to the restricted fiche. The argument they want to see is how the intent of the action has been met in the soldier's career. If someone gave you a letter of reprimand and requested that it be filed in your performance fiche, he or she probably intended for it to slow down or stop your career. You have to convince the board either that the action was completely unfounded or that justice has been served. The unfounded issue is hard to prove on an administrative issue, because the person who gave it to you is considered to have already examined the issues and determined that a reasonable condition existed. Make sure you address the right issue, and use the wording in the regulations to enforce your argument.

You can refer to the sample letter as a guide for either board. The letter from your legal assistance lawyer should accompany a letter of this type from the chain of command. Your best resource is the Legal Assistance Office and intervention from your chain of command. Get them on your team.

RCP

This section is for soldiers who are being forced out because they are exceeding their retention control point (RCP) for their grade. Currently, a specialist or corporal in the Army can remain on active duty for eight years as long as he or she is in a promotable status. At eight years of service they are discharged. A promotable SGT has to make SSG by his fifteenth year of service. There should be no reason for a soldier not to be promoted by his RCP date. If you are nearing one of those critical junctures, put your career progression motor into overdrive and do whatever it takes to get promoted. Several ideas to accelerate your career are presented throughout this book. However, they must be implemented prior to one's RCP date. If they are not and this date passes, there is no solution.

Through no fault of your own, you may have incorrect records that have prevented you from getting a promotion you rightfully deserve. The Army has an old philosophy that goes something like this: Soldiers are responsible for their own records and are to blame for unresolved issues.

(Letterhead)

(Office Symbol)   (Date)

MEMORANDUM FOR: Enlisted Evaluations and Review Board

SUBJECT: Action to Move an Administrative Letter of Reprimand
                from the Performance Fiche to the Restricted Fiche on SGT
                Allen M. Becker

1. Your office is currently working on a decision involving one of the soldiers in my command, Sergeant Allen M. Becker. My concern is that
   SGT Becker's military career will be unnecessarily destroyed by an
   administrative letter of reprimand that is based on an NCOER that was
   recently overturned (see attached copy). It is my firm belief that SGT
   Becker is an outstanding noncommissioned officer who is being pun-
   ished for a crime that was alleged against him without any substantiated
   proof. This letter of reprimand was given to him as an administrative
   action because there is no legal requirement for a burden of proof associated with administrative actions. SGT Becker would have been
   charged under the Uniform Code of Military Justice (UCMJ) had there
   been any real evidence against him.

2. SGT Becker is being considered for elimination from the Army based
   solely on this letter of reprimand and the associated NCOER. Mrs.
   Somebody from the QMP board said the actions against SGT Becker
   would stop once she receives faxed confirmation of the overturned
   NCOER and a copy of your office's action to place this letter of reprimand into SGT Becker's restricted fiche.

3. This case is unique because it involves a professional noncommissioned officer who has a military file and performance of duty history that
   is absolutely remarkable! SGT Becker was a three-time select for NCO
   of the cycle during his $2^1/_2$ years teaching at the NCO academy. He is
   an extremely dedicated and motivated NCO who deserves fair and ratio-
   nal treatment that is based on a known performance history and not on
   conjecture.

4. I request that you please grant this command request on SGT Becker's
   behalf. This request is made based on my belief that anything less
   would ruin his Army career and not be justified based on his exemplary
   background. In addition, please note carefully the letter from SGT
   Becker that the legal assistance attorneys helped him write. Their legal
   interpretation of this administrative action is noteworthy. Please feel free
   to call me at DSN 123-456/6789 or commercial at (123) 456-7890 for
   any further information and/or assistance. Thank you for your attention
   to this case.

                                    Commander's Name
                                    CPT, Branch
                                    Commanding

Sample Letter from Chain of Command to Fix a QMP Action

Keep in mind that the Army trains personnel records clerks for only eight weeks to qualify them to work on a soldier's records. Then the clerks are sent to their duty assignments to spend a year or two learning everything that was not taught to them in school. The chances of errors being made are high and probable.

The soldier should be the person most interested in his or her own record and related career progression. Unfortunately, even first sergeants often don't know a lot about their soldiers' records. Knowing this should make every soldier personally invested in keeping good track of his or her own records. No one else is as interested in your career as you!

Chain-of-Command Involvement

Probably every unit in the Army has soldiers with hidden problems in their records that may be keeping them from being rightfully promoted. For those in the chain of command, there is the added responsibility of dealing with this. The only way to find the problems and to aid the soldiers is to scrub 201 files and promotion packets and to conduct personal interviews.

Your soldier may have had his or her promotion packet prepared by an inexperienced records clerk who perhaps was not as alert or caring as he or she should have been. Or possibly the orderly room or S-1 section may be missing important soldier care issues. Whatever the cause, there are definitely problem records throughout the Army. That specialist that is exceeding his retention control point may have made the previous cutoff score had the records been correctly managed. A caring chain of command will stay abreast of changing promotion criteria and make a point of regularly checking on soldiers' records and promotion packets.

It should be an important unit goal to educate soldiers in the proper upkeep of their military records. Classes can be given by the records section of your local Personnel Office. Invite the counselors from the Education Center into your unit areas to brief on current opportunities for promotion. Keep an eye out for stellar performers who just might make good warrants or commissioned officers.

The sample letter demonstrates just how important screening can be if done before a soldier is forced out. Leaders should survey their soldiers and their records to prevent occurrences of this magnitude. Leadership intervention can keep otherwise good soldiers in the Army and conserve our valuable training resources. The Personnel Background/Skills Survey is provided as a sample tool that can be used to assess individual talent and career progression needs.

(Letterhead)

(Office Symbol)   (Date)

MEMORANDUM FOR: Enlisted Promotions Branch

SUBJECT: Promotion Point Adjustment (Retroactive) for
         SPC (P) Robert M. Tanner

1. Request that SPC Tanner's promotion packet be adjusted to reflect
    67 additional points that should have been in his file since his last
    official recomputation of November 2001.

2. I discovered inconsistencies between SPC Tanner's 201 file and
    his perceived promotion potential during my initial command inter-
    view with him on 26 September 2002. I took command of Bravo
    Battery on 1 September 2002 and have been conducting record
    reviews and personal interviews with each Bravo Battery soldier
    since my change of command. His answers to questions regarding
    his 201 file prompted me to research even deeper into his promo-
    tion packet history. I discovered several major errors in his packet
    that were generated by the unit, the S-1, and the Enlisted Promo-
    tions Section.

3. These errors have had a significant negative impact on SPC Tan-
    ner's career potential. He is currently scheduled to ETS on 4
    November 2003 because he will have eight years of enlisted ser-
    vice and will have reached his retention control point (RCP) for his
    grade. If these 67 points had been in his record in November 2001,
    he would have been promoted to E-5 in February 2002, when the
    points for his MOS (16T) dropped to 572.

4. The 16T MOS (Patriot crew member) is a shortage MOS for the
    Army, and especially so at the E-5/E-6 grade levels. Our battalion
    is currently briefing the 16T MOS shortage as a critical shortage on
    all of our quarterly and yearly training briefs. His promotion would
    fulfill a critical position shortage for the unit and help rectify prob-
    lems that were generated during the previous unit's administration
    (the soldier's platoon sergeant, 1SG, and commander have all
    been in the unit less than ninety days).

Sample Request for Retroactive Promotion Point Adjustment

5. The problems associated with his packet are as follows:

    (1)   The soldier was not notified of his recomputation.

    (2)   A current PT score was not included in the recomputation figures, even though the soldier had taken two valid PT tests during the previous year.

    (3)   An ARCOM Medal was not transferred to the recomputation worksheet by the Enlisted Promotions Branch personnel, even though one was listed on the original worksheet.

    (4)   Twenty-two credit hours of college credit were not placed in the soldier's promotion packet (shown on attached copy of transcript). This is a twofold problem, because the soldier could have generated a transcript for his file if he had known that he was going to be recomped (credit granted prior month).

    (5)   The 10 additional points for educational improvement were not added, based on the same reason previously stated.

    (6)   The unit commander did not sign the recomputation worksheet (we don't know whether he saw it or not).

    (7)   No follow-up work was done at the unit and/or S-1 level.

6. SPC Tanner is a good soldier. His unit performance has been outstanding, and he is currently filling an E-5 slot. His record shows that he has many valuable experiences, including Desert Storm, helicopter repair, wheeled vehicle repair, Patriot missile, and a year of college. He has received numerous awards and has a reputation as an energetic worker. He has already demonstrated his ability to lead soldiers and definitely wants to continue his career in the Army.

7. Please expedite this request for a promotion point adjustment to SPC Tanner's packet. A favorable action on this request will allow the Army to keep a well-trained and motivated soldier on active duty. His ETS date and RCP are approaching fast, and a decisive answer is needed soon. The POC for any additional information will be the undersigned at DSN 123-4567.

                        Commander's Name
                        CPT, Branch
                        Commanding

Sample Request for Retroactive Promotion Point Adjustment
continued

PERSONNEL BACKGROUND/SKILLS SURVEY

Name _____ Rank _____ DOR ____ Reserve rank ____

SSN _____ DOB _____ ETS _____ PCS _____ MOS _____

Other MOSs held _____ Additional Skill Identifiers(ASI) _____

Promotable status (Y/N) ____ GT score _____ SQT/SDT score & date _____

Please list the activities, hobbies, and/or sports events that most interest you.
(*Be specific, e.g., baseball, art crafts, motorcycle racing, wood crafts, etc.*)

_____

_____

_____

_____

Do you have any additional language skills? (*for example, Spanish, French, etc.*) _____

Have you ever taken the Defense Language Aptitude Test (DLAT)? _____

If so, what was your score?_____

Is English your primary language? _____

High school/GED (yes/no) _____

Year graduated/completed _____

What college courses have you taken? _____

Degree(s) held_____

Colleges and/or universities attended _____

_____

Have you ever taken any postsecondary tests? (*for example, CLEP, DANTES, SST, and/or ASE*)

Please list all that you've taken and if you passed them. (*P or F*)

_____

_____

What military awards do you have? (*Be specific and include the number of each award.*) _____

_____

Have you ever received certificates of achievement and/or letters of recommendation, etc.? _____

_____

Have you ever participated in any type of board? (*Examples would include promotion boards, NCO of the month/quarter boards, practice boards, etc.*) List any boards that you have been to. _____

_____

Have you ever given any classes and/or been asked to present information?

_____

What correspondence courses have you taken? _____

_____

_____

Did you complete them? _____

What military schools/courses have you taken? (*Include length in weeks of course.*) _____

_____

_____

_____

_____

_____

Have you ever had your military schooling accredited by a college and/or university? _____

What are your career goals? (*Be specific, and include civilian career goals if you have any.*) _____

_____

_____

_____

_____

Are you enrolled in any type of educational fund? (*e.g., VEAP, GI Bill, etc.*)

_____

Have you talked with an educational counselor about your career/educational goals? _____

When was the last time you talked with a counselor? _____

Have you ever had career guidance counseling from the leadership in your chain of command? _____

When was the last time you were counseled? (*approximate month and year*)

_____

Why did you join the Army? _____

_____

_____

_____

What do you like best about the Army? _____

_____

What do you dislike about the Army? _____

_____

12

Why Set Goals?

Judging from their reluctance to set goals, many people must believe that goal setting has no real lasting value as a tool to further their careers. Some would argue that their personal and professional goals are firmly established in their minds and that they constantly think about them and make decisions in accordance with them. In reality, however, most people are much too busy to really be so effective. Day-to-day pressures tend to drive people more than their perceived goals do. Establishing written goals will help you determine your future paths more firmly.

In today's hectic world, there are countless things that weigh on our minds and compete for our time. Any given day holds "important" activities that vie for our attention. Most people would agree that they rarely complete everything they want to in a given day or week. This must mean that some things are left undone. Unfortunately, often the easiest things to leave undone are those things that are the most important to an individual or would give him or her the most future success. Priorities need to be set as to which things get accomplished. Written goals that are reviewed frequently force you to constantly assess the importance and relevance of each activity. Following is an example of how well-written goals can work for you.

A NEW SOLDIER TAKES CHARGE OF HIS CAREER
Private Blake has just purchased a copy of this book as reading material for the plane ride to his first duty station. He is excited about the possibility of getting promoted to E-5 quickly. After reading this chapter, he writes down some of his goals for the coming year:
- Complete four correspondence courses valued at 30 points or more.
- Take two college classes and get my military training evaluated onto an AARTS transcript.
- Study for and take a minimum of twenty-five CLEP, DANTES, or SST equivalency exams.
- Score a minimum of 270 on my next and subsequent PT tests.
- Find a topic and write an interesting unit-related story for a local paper.

- Commit to being the best and sharpest saluter in the unit.
- Complete one extra project per week at the next unit under my own initiative.
- Find a way to use my "hidden" expertise in automotive maintenance to help the unit.
- Review my goals at least twice daily throughout the next year.

   Private Blake's goals may seem rather lofty. After all, he is just a brand-new private. Can he really expect to do all of these things? These goals may seem extravagant at first glance, but when broken down into smaller bites, they actually are very manageable. Following is how he might break this list down into smaller, more readily achievable short-term goals.

Short-Term Goals

- Complete four correspondence courses valued at 30 points or more.
    - —Go to education center and sign up for one correspondence course.
    - —Call Correspondence Course Center and ask for bulk shipment of books.
- Take two college classes and get my military training evaluated onto a transcript.
    - —Visit Education Center and fill out AARTS transcript request form.
    - —Go to Enlisted Records Section and get copies of personnel files.
    - —Sign up for college class and enroll with institution.
- Study for and take a minimum of twenty-five CLEP, DANTES, or SST equivalency exams.
    - —Review lists of currently available tests at Education Center.
    - —Take two pretests per week.
    - —Take one real test per week.
    - —Study at least one hour per night for each test taken.
- Score a minimum of 270 on my next and subsequent PT tests.
    - —Review requirements for 90-percent pass rate in each of three events.
    - —Increase push-up and sit-up routine by five additional practice reps per week.
- Find a topic and write an interesting unit-related story for a local paper.
    - —Look for things the unit does very well.
    - —Visit the local military paper office and ask questions about topics wanted.
- Commit to being the best and sharpest saluter in the unit.
    - —Learn unit slogan.
    - —Practice salute and motivated voice.
    - —Salute and sound off from greater distance than required by regulation.
    - —Look for opportunities to exercise military courtesy beyond normal expectations.

- Complete one extra project per week at the next unit under my own initiative.
  —Concentrate on accomplishing quality missions in less time than peers.
  —Seek projects normally executed by higher-ranking personnel or often left undone.
  —Stay after work at least twice per week to do other work.
- Find a way to use my "hidden" expertise in automotive maintenance to help the unit.
  —Possibly use automotive knowledge during after-duty hours with unit mechanics.
- Review my goals at least twice daily throughout the next year.
  —Review goals every morning before going to work.
  —Convert big goals into smaller daily, weekly, and monthly goals.
  —Write goals on a calendar or to-do list.
  —Review accomplishments before going to bed each night.

Now it should be more evident how writing down goals can help you achieve more long-term success. Seeing these things on paper makes it easier to break them into manageable pieces. As the old saying goes, "How do you eat an elephant? One bite at a time!"

What should be most evident is that Private Blake is not going to be a private for very long. It is rare to find soldiers who plan to excel in this way. Those who do always stand out from their peers. Try a similar plan, and you'll reap great benefits in your career progression goals or other initiatives.

STUDY TESTS AND OTHER TOOLS FOR HELP WITH GOALS

Another excellent technique for goal setting is to evaluate the potential goals from the perspective of the test itself and/or the process used by the Army for giving credit. For instance, a review of the Record Fire Scorecard (DA Form 3595-R) shows how the firing requirements and expectations are scored to include the time in seconds to respond to each target on the firing range as well as the distance to the targets. A careful review of these types of aspects can help the soldier mentally prepare to do better at the firing range and thus score higher for the qualification and subsequent points awarded for promotion.

The same realities can be observed through the Combat Pistol Qualification Course Scorecard (DA Form 88-R), the Scaled Target Alternate Course (DA Form 5790-R), and the Army Physical Fitness Test Scorecard (DA Form 705). *See forms that follow.*

RECORD FIRE SCORECARD

For use of this form see FM 3-22.9; the proponent agency is TRADOC.

ID CODE	UNIT	DATE (YYYYMMDD)	EVALUATOR'S ID CODE

TABLE 1 — PRONE SUPPORTED OR FOXHOLE SUPPORTED FIRING POSITION

RD	RANGE (m)	TIME (sec)	HIT	MISS	NO FIRE	RD	RANGE (m)	TIME (sec)	HIT	MISS	NO FIRE
1	50	3				11	100	8			
2	200	6				12	200				
3	100	4				13	150	10			
4	150	5				14	300				
5	300	8				15	100	9			
6	250	7				16	250				
7	50	3				17	200	6			
8	200	6				18	150	5			
9	150	5				19	50	6			
10	250	7				20	100				
							TOTAL				

TABLE 2 — PRONE UNSUPPORTED FIRING POSITION

RD	RANGE (m)	TIME (sec)	HIT	MISS	NO FIRE
1	200	6			
2	250	8			
3	150	6			
4	300	10			
5	200				
6	150				
7	200	12			
8	250				
9	150	9			
10	150	6			
TOTAL					

TABLE 3 — KNEELING UNSUPPORTED FIRING POSITION

RD	RANGE (m)	TIME (sec)	HIT	MISS	NO FIRE
1	150	8			
2	50	4			
3	100	5			
4	150	6			
5	100	5			
6	50	4			
7	100	5			
8	150	6			
9	50	4			
10	100	5			
TOTAL					

QUALIFICATION SCORE RATINGS (Check One)

☐ 36-40 -- EXPERT	☐ 23-29 -- MARKSMAN
☐ 30-35 -- SHARPSHOOTER	☐ 22 AND BELOW -- UNQUALIFIED

SCORE

TABLE	HIT	MISS	NO FIRE
1			
2			
3			

FIRER'S QUALIFICATION SCORE

Qualified with IBA? ☐ YES ☐ NO

AIMING DEVICE USED (Check One)

☐ IRON SIGHT	☐ AN/PAS-13 (DAY)
☐ BACKUP IRON SIGHT	☐ AN/PAS-13 (NIGHT)
☐ M68, CCO	☐ AN/PAQ-4B/C
☐ ACOG	☐ AN/PEQ-2A/B

REMARKS

NIGHT FIRE EXERCISE

HIT	MISS	GO	NO GO
		☐	☐

DATE (YYYYMMDD)

CBRN FIRE EXERCISE

HIT	MISS	GO	NO GO
		☐	☐

DATE (YYYYMMDD)

SCORER'S INITIALS	DATE INITIALED (YYYYMMDD)
OFFICER'S INITIALS	DATE INITIALED (YYYYMMDD)

Record Fire Scorecard

The record fire course provides for the engagement of one 20-round exercise and two 10-round exercises. Soldiers engage 20 single or multiple targets from the prone supported or foxhole supported firing position, 10 targets from the prone unsupported firing position, and 10 targets from the kneeling unsupported firing position. Once firing begins, crossloading of ammunition is not allowed. The uniform for qualification is a helmet, LBE/LBV, and interceptor body armor with front and back SAPI plates (if available). No other armor is required.

(1) Table 1 -- Prone Supported Firing Position (or at the unit commander's discretion) Foxhole Supported Firing Position. The firer is given one 20-round magazine to engage 20 targets at various ranges.

(2) Table 2 -- Prone Unsupported Firing Position. The firer is given one 10-round magazine to engage 10 targets at various ranges.

(3) Table 3 -- Kneeling Unsupported Firing Position. The firer is given one 10-round magazine to engage 10 targets at various ranges.

(4) Credit for target hits should not be given when rounds are "saved" from difficult targets for use on easier targets (for example, not firing at the 300-meter target so an additional round can be fired at the 150-meter target). When double targets are exposed, the Soldier should fire two rounds. If he misses the first target, he may fire at that same target with the second round.

(5) Soldiers should engage the target that poses the greatest threat first (normally assumed to be the closer target). No scoring distinction is made between near and far targets or the sequence in which the Soldier engages them. Credit is not given if unused ammunition from one 20-round table is added to a magazine provided for the next table.

(6) Soldiers who fail to qualify on the first attempt should be given appropriate remedial training and allowed to refire in a few days. When a soldier refires the course, he remains unqualified with a score of 22 target hits or less. A rating of marksman is awarded for a score of 23 to 40 target hits. When automated scoring procedures that allow a Soldier's performance to be stored and retrieved before a weapon malfunction are available, his performance is added to the score of his first attempt after weapon repair and refire. If a Soldier's weapon becomes inoperable and his performance before a malfunction precludes qualification, he is considered unqualified and must refire.

(7) Alibi firing is reserved for soldiers who encounter a malfunctioning target, ammunition, or rifle. A soldier will not be issued more than 20 rounds for Table 1, 10 rounds for Table 2, and 10 rounds for Table 3. Soldiers who fire 20 rounds despite a target malfunction will not be issued additional alibi rounds. There are no alibis for Soldier-induced weapon malfunctions or for targets missed during application of immediate action. These procedures must be strictly adhered to when a malfunction occurs.

Record Fire Scorecard *continued*

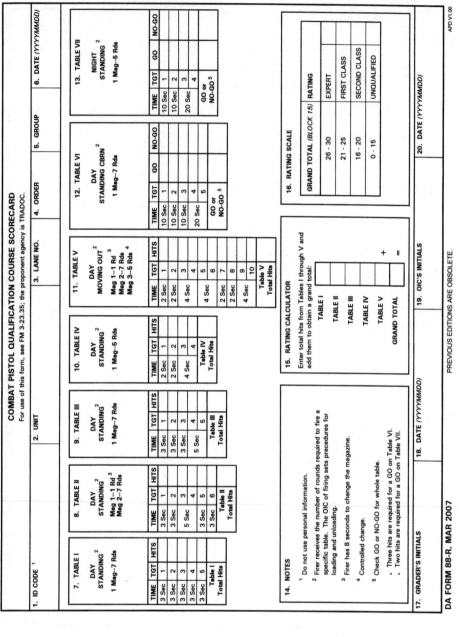

COMBAT PISTOL QUALIFICATION COURSE SCORECARD

For use of this form, see FM 3-23.35; the proponent agency is TRADOC.

1. ID CODE [1]	2. UNIT	3. LANE NO.	4. ORDER	5. GROUP	6. DATE *(YYYYMMDD)*

7. TABLE I
DAY STANDING [2]
1 Mag—7 Rds

TIME	TGT	HITS
3 Sec	1	
3 Sec	2	
3 Sec	3	
3 Sec	4	
3 Sec	5	
Table I Total Hits		

8. TABLE II
DAY STANDING [2]
Mag 1—1 Rd [3]
Mag 2—7 Rds

TIME	TGT	HITS
3 Sec	1	
3 Sec	2	
5 Sec	3	
5 Sec	4	
3 Sec	5	
3 Sec	6	
Table II Total Hits		

9. TABLE III
DAY STANDING [2]
1 Mag—7 Rds

TIME	TGT	HITS
3 Sec	1	
3 Sec	2	
3 Sec	3	
5 Sec	4	
5 Sec	5	
Table III Total Hits		

10. TABLE IV
DAY STANDING [2]
1 Mag—5 Rds

TIME	TGT	HITS
2 Sec	1	
2 Sec	2	
4 Sec	3	
Table IV Total Hits		

11. TABLE V
DAY MOVING OUT [2]
Mag 1—1 Rd [3]
Mag 2—7 Rds [3]
Mag 3—5 Rds [4]

TIME	TGT	HITS
2 Sec	1	
2 Sec	2	
4 Sec	3	
4 Sec	4	
4 Sec	5	
4 Sec	6	
2 Sec	7	
2 Sec	8	
4 Sec	9	
4 Sec	10	
Table V Total Hits		

12. TABLE VI
DAY STANDING CBRN [2]
1 Mag—7 Rds

TIME	TGT	GO	NO-GO
10 Sec	1		
10 Sec	2		
10 Sec	3		
20 Sec	4		
20 Sec	5		
GO or NO-GO [5]			

13. TABLE VII
NIGHT STANDING [2]
1 Mag—5 Rds

TIME	TGT	GO	NO-GO
10 Sec	1		
10 Sec	2		
20 Sec	3		
20 Sec	4		
GO or NO-GO [5]			

14. NOTES

[1] Do not use personal information.

[2] Firer receives the number of rounds required to fire a specific table. The OIC of firing sets precedures for loading and unloading.

[3] Firer has 8 seconds to change the magazine.

[4] Controlled change.

[5] Check GO or NO-GO for whole table.
- Three hits are required for a GO on Table VI.
- Two hits are required for a GO on Table VII.

15. RATING CALCULATOR

Enter total hits from Tables I through V and add them to obtain a grand total:

TABLE I	
TABLE II	
TABLE III	
TABLE IV	
TABLE V	+
GRAND TOTAL	=

16. RATING SCALE

GRAND TOTAL *(BLOCK 15)*	RATING
26 - 30	EXPERT
21 - 25	FIRST CLASS
16 - 20	SECOND CLASS
0 - 15	UNQUALIFIED

17. GRADER'S INITIALS	18. DATE *(YYYYMMDD)*	19. OIC'S INITIALS	20. DATE *(YYYYMMDD)*

DA FORM 88-R, MAR 2007   PREVIOUS EDITIONS ARE OBSOLETE.   APD v1.00

Combat Pistol Qualification Course Scorecard

RECORD FIRING SCORECARD -- SCALED TARGET ALTERNATE COURSE

For use of this form, see FM 3-22.9; the proponent agency is TRADOC.

ID CODE (NOT SSN)	UNIT	DATE (YYYYMMDD)	EVALUATOR'S ID CODE (NOT SSN)

TABLE 1 — PRONE SUPPORTED OR FOXHOLE SUPPORTED FIRING POSITION (TIME: 120 SECONDS)

RD	RANGE (m)	HIT	MISS
1	300		
2	300		
3	250		
4	250		
5	200		
6	200		
7	200		
8	200		
9	150		
10	150		
11	150		
12	150		
13	100		
14	100		
15	100		
16	100		
17	100		
18	100		
19	50		
20	50		
TOTAL			

TABLE 2 — PRONE UNSUPPORTED FIRING POSITION (TIME: 60 SECONDS)

RD	RANGE (m)	HIT	MISS
1	300		
2	250		
3	200		
4	200		
5	150		
6	150		
7	100		
8	100		
9	100		
10	50		
TOTAL			

TABLE 3 — KNEELING FIRING POSITION (TIME: 60 SECONDS)

RD	RANGE (m)	HIT	MISS
1	150		
2	150		
3	100		
4	100		
5	100		
6	100		
7	100		
8	100		
9	50		
10	50		
TOTAL			

REMARKS: FIRER ISSUED 40 ROUNDS TO ENGAGE 10 TARGETS. THE ROUNDS WILL BE PRELOADED IN ONE 20-ROUND MAGAZINE FOR TABLE 1, ONE 10-ROUND MAGAZINE FOR TABLE 2, AND ONE 10-ROUND MAGAZINE FOR TABLE 3.

QUALIFICATION SCORE RATINGS (Check One)

- [ ] 36-40 -- EXPERT
- [ ] 30-35 -- SHARPSHOOTER
- [ ] 23-29 -- MARKSMAN
- [ ] 22 AND BELOW -- UNQUALIFIED

SCORE

TABLE	HIT	MISS	NO FIRE
1			
2			
3			

FIRER'S QUALIFICATION SCORE

NIGHT FIRE EXERCISE

DATE (YYYYMMDD)	HIT	MISS	GO	NO GO

CBRN FIRE EXERCISE

DATE (YYYYMMDD)	HIT	MISS	GO	NO GO

REMARKS

SCORER'S INITIALS	DATE INITIALED (YYYYMMDD)
OFFICER'S INITIALS	DATE INITIALED (YYYYMMDD)

DA FORM 5790-R, JAN 2011   PREVIOUS EDITIONS ARE OBSOLETE.

Record Firing Scorecard * Scaled Target Alternate Course

This scorecard is used to score alternate course record fire qualification when the 25-meter scaled silhouette target (NSN 6920-01-167-1398) is used. The alternate course is used only when standard record fire and known distance ranges are unavailable.

NOTE: If zeroing/grouping exercises are not performed on the day of record fire, six rounds of training/sustainment ammunition will be fired for 25-meter zero confirmation prior to conducting the qualification course.

CONDUCT OF FIRE

Alternate course qualification firers will have one 20-round magazine and two 10-round magazines. To ensure that firers do not forget which targets they engaged and shoot a given target more than the prescribed number of times, firers should adhere to the following guideline: Engage targets on the sheet from left to right and nearest to farthest. Engagement should follow this order: 50m, 100m left, 100m center, 100m right, 150m left, 150m right, 200m left, 200m right, 250m, and 300m.

Though the time between each firing position is not specified, enough time should be allotted to allow the firer to clear his weapon, quickly change firing positions, and reload before beginning the next firing table. The range RSO ensures that enough time is given between each change in firing position to facilitate the timely flow of the record fire qualification table.

(1) Table 1 -- Prone Supported Firing Position or (at the unit commander's discretion) Foxhole Supported Firing Position.
The firer is given one 20-round magazine to engage 10 silhouettes on the same target sheet. Table 1 includes 2 rounds for each silhouette. Firing must be completed in 120 seconds. No more than 2 hits are scored for each silhouette.

(2) Table 2 -- Prone Unsupported Firing Position.
The firer is given one 10-round magazine to engage 10 silhouettes on the same target sheet. Table 2 includes 1 round for each silhouette. Firing must be completed in 60 seconds. No more than 1 hit is scored for each silhouette.

(3) Table 3 -- Kneeling Firing Position.
The firer is given one 10-round magazine to engage 10 silhouettes on the target sheet. Table 3 includes 2 rounds for each silhouette positioned at 50 and 100 meters and 1 round for each silhouette positioned at 150 meters. Firing must be completed in 60 seconds. No more than 2 hits are scored for the 50- and 100-meter silhouettes, and 1 hit is scored for each 150-meter silhouette.

SCORING

The same target sheet is used for every 40-round qualification table that a firer completes. One hit is awarded for each round that strikes within or touches some part of the silhouette. A maximum of 40 hits is comprised of 3 hits per target at 200, 250, and 300 meters; 4 hits per target at 150 meters; and 5 hits per target at 50 and 100 meters.

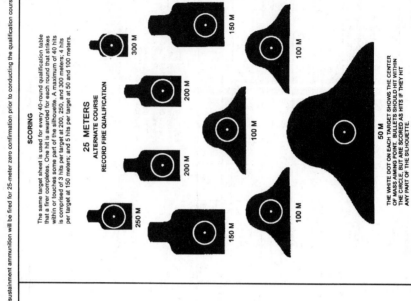

25 METERS
ALTERNATE COURSE
RECORD FIRE QUALIFICATION

THE WHITE DOT ON EACH TARGET SHOWS THE CENTER OF MASS AIMING POINT. BULLETS SHOULD HIT WITHIN THE CIRCLE, BUT ARE SCORED AS HITS IF THEY HIT ANY PART OF THE SILHOUETTE.

DA FORM 5790-R, JAN 2011

Record Firing Scorecard * Scaled Target Alternate Course *continued*

Army Physical Fitness Test Scorecard

For use of this form, see FM 7-22; the proponent agency is TRADOC.

NAME (Last, First, MI)

GENDER

UNIT

TEST ONE

DATE	GRADE	AGE

HEIGHT (IN INCHES)	BODY COMPOSITION		
	WEIGHT: ___ lbs GO / NO-GO ☐	BODY FAT: ___ % GO / NO-GO ☐	

PU RAW SCORE	INITIALS	POINTS
SU RAW SCORE	INITIALS	POINTS
2MR RAW SCORE	INITIALS	POINTS
ALTERNATE AEROBIC EVENT		TOTAL POINTS

EVENT ___

TIME ___

GO ☐ NO-GO ☐

NCOIC/OIC SIGNATURE

COMMENTS

TEST TWO

DATE	GRADE	AGE

HEIGHT (IN INCHES)	BODY COMPOSITION		
	WEIGHT: ___ lbs GO / NO-GO ☐	BODY FAT: ___ % GO / NO-GO ☐	

PU RAW SCORE	INITIALS	POINTS
SU RAW SCORE	INITIALS	POINTS
2MR RAW SCORE	INITIALS	POINTS
ALTERNATE AEROBIC EVENT		TOTAL POINTS

EVENT ___

TIME ___

GO ☐ NO-GO ☐

NCOIC/OIC SIGNATURE

COMMENTS

TEST THREE

DATE	GRADE	AGE

HEIGHT (IN INCHES)	BODY COMPOSITION		
	WEIGHT: ___ lbs GO / NO-GO ☐	BODY FAT: ___ % GO / NO-GO ☐	

PU RAW SCORE	INITIALS	POINTS
SU RAW SCORE	INITIALS	POINTS
2MR RAW SCORE	INITIALS	POINTS
ALTERNATE AEROBIC EVENT		TOTAL POINTS

EVENT ___

TIME ___

GO ☐ NO-GO ☐

NCOIC/OIC SIGNATURE

COMMENTS

TEST FOUR

DATE	GRADE	AGE

HEIGHT (IN INCHES)	BODY COMPOSITION		
	WEIGHT: ___ lbs GO / NO-GO ☐	BODY FAT: ___ % GO / NO-GO ☐	

PU RAW SCORE	INITIALS	POINTS
SU RAW SCORE	INITIALS	POINTS
2MR RAW SCORE	INITIALS	POINTS
ALTERNATE AEROBIC EVENT		TOTAL POINTS

EVENT ___

TIME ___

GO ☐ NO-GO ☐

NCOIC/OIC SIGNATURE

COMMENTS

SPECIAL INSTRUCTION: USE INK

LEGEND: PU - PUSH UPS   2MR - 2 MILE RUN
         SU - SIT UPS   APFT - ARMY PHYSICAL FITNESS TEST

DA FORM 705, MAY 2010   PREVIOUS EDITIONS ARE OBSOLETE.   APD LC v1.03ES

Army Physical Fitness Test Scorecard

13

Special Advice for Anyone Considering Joining the Army

WHY THE MILITARY IS AN EXCELLENT CAREER CHOICE
For those on the outside, the Army or military may seem to be a daunting career choice full of unknown possibilities. The reality of military service is that it can be a very fun and rewarding career with lots of exciting choices for what to do, where to go, and how long to stay.

Regardless of where you are in that decision-making process, it is important to recognize that the Army or military environment can be an excellent career choice, whether you spend three years or thirty in the service. That said, the decision to join and what choices to make before and after joining can make all the difference in the world in your career progression pathway.

Statistically speaking, most soldiers spend only a few years serving in the military and then move on to other career fields after serving honorably for three or more years. Some, like the author, join thinking it is a good choice for earning college credit and gaining solid experience, and later decide to continue their career until retirement.

Whichever road chosen, most of the current and former soldiers have undoubtedly gained a wealth of experiences that will serve them well for the remainder of their adult lives. The military is an honored profession and it helps shape ordinary citizens into great leaders in every field of endeavor imaginable. Whether you want to be a mechanic or a surgeon, the Army can provide an excellent platform for becoming the best person you can possibly be.

Years ago, the Army had a recruiting slogan that said "The Army does more before 9:00 a.m. than most people do all day." Although not entirely true, it did capture a realistic picture of soldiers being involved in daily duties and missions that propelled them into exciting activities and learning experiences that are hard to imagine as a civilian citizen.

The remainder of this chapter will focus on how you can better analyze and weigh the differences between military and civilian life and help you make career decisions that may or may not include serving in the Army or one of the other armed services. It is the author's hope that those who decide to serve in the Army will have a much better start to their military career thanks to the insights found in this book.

PROMOTION POINTERS BEFORE YOU JOIN

There are lots of opportunities for career progression within the military environment. It is a wide-open field for virtually any direction of learning and area of interest and it offers exciting choices. That said, there are definitely some questions and topics that should be discussed with a military recruiter before signing on the proverbial dotted line.

There is a saying in the debating world: "He who asks the question, wins the debate." That axiom bears some weight in the recruiting world too. There are an unbelievable amount of career choices that can be made long before the young soldier begins his or her journey in the Army. Those choices can lead to either a wide-open and fast-paced career journey or to a slower-paced and sometimes frustrating career pathway.

You should ask your recruiter the right questions, and therefore own more of the process. You must take the right steps to ensure both the short-term and long-term success of your military career journey. One of the more critical initial tasks is to make sure you get credit for anything for which you might be eligible, as such credit can count toward a higher entry rank, a special training or education path, or recognition of a skill you earned prior to beginning active duty.

For instance, part of the recruitment process will be taking tests to determine the level of aptitude you have for different training and career options. These tests are critical because your scores may provide you with a lot of latitude in your career choices. That doesn't mean the recruiter will necessarily address your qualifications and options to the full degree that may be warranted by your entry file.

It is important to understand that there may be conflicting issues that recruiting personnel face that may or may not benefit your scores. For instance, they may be dealing with the need to fill a critical shortage of personnel in a particular field. Perhaps the Army is critically short of mechanics and your test results show you have the aptitude to do well in that field. That doesn't mean you don't have the aptitude and ability to do just as well or better in another field or military occupational specialty.

THE EXTRA VALUE OF MILITARY EXPERIENCE

America's military forces are equipped with some of the best technology, training, and resources available anywhere in the world. Soldiers are integrated into a career field that exposes them to some of the best and most unique lifetime experiences imaginable. There is also a strong family-like camaraderie that permeates military life and builds strong bonds that outlast the bonds of many other career choices.

The military is also a resource for education and training that is second to none. The experiences gained while serving in the Army or other military service can be very difficult to match anywhere else. For instance, soldiers often are issued equipment, vehicles, and gear worth hundreds of thousands of dollars—and sometimes millions of dollars—to be used in the course of their normal day-to-day jobs.

Young soldiers and leaders are also given responsibilities that allow them to achieve goals that they might never have achieved otherwise. The military is a great training ground for performance-based achievement, and those achievements tend to build both the character and the leadership qualities of the individual soldier. These aspects of normal military life are worth their weight in gold for an aspiring man or woman with the vision and desire to improve him- or herself through hard work and personal or team accomplishments.

The Army or military environment can also be a great place to figure out what you want to do with your life. Many young people in American society struggle with career direction and focus and often find it difficult to choose a definitive career path while in high school or college. The exciting and varied missions of military life make it easier for many to discover things about themselves or things about career choices that may have eluded them before joining the military.

Sources

ARMY REGULATIONS (AR)
AR 27-10, Military Justice
AR 135-100, Appointment of Commissioned and Warrant Officers of the Army
AR 135-178, Enlisted Administrative Separations
AR 135-205, Enlisted Personnel Management
AR 145-1, Senior ROTC Program: Organization, Administration, and Training
AR 195-6, Department of the Army Polygraph Activities
AR 350-1, Army Training and Leader Development
AR 350-6, Army-Wide Small Arms Competitive Marksmanship
AR 350-17, NCO Development Program
AR 350-41, Training in Units
AR 351-1, Individual Military Education and Training
AR 351-5, US Army Officer Candidate School
AR 351-12, Nomination to the US Army Military Academy: Enlisted Categories; Army
AR 600-8-2, Suspension of Favorable Personnel Actions (Flags)
AR 600-9, The Army Body Composition Program
AR 600-20, Army Command Policy
AR 600-37, Unfavorable Information
AR 601-280, Army Retention Program
AR 608-50, Legal Assistance
AR 611-112, Personnel Selection and Classification, Manual of Warrant Officer MOSs
AR 611-201, Enlisted Career Management Fields and Military Occupational Specialty
AR 614-200, Enlisted Assignments and Utilization Management
AR 621-5, Army Continuing Education System (ACES)
AR 621-6, Army Learning Centers
AR 621-202, Army Educational Incentives and Entitlements
AR 623-205, Enlisted Evaluation Report
AR 635-200, Active-Duty Enlisted Administrative Separations
AR 640-2-1, Personnel Qualification Records
AR 640-10, Individual Military Personnel Records
AR 670-1, Wear and Appearance of Army Uniforms and Insignia
AR 672-5-1, Awards and Decorations

ARMY TECHNIQUES PUBLICATION
ATP 6-22.1, The Counseling Process

DEPARTMENT OF THE ARMY CIRCULAR
DA Circular 601-99-1, Warrant Officer Procurement Program

DEPARTMENT OF THE ARMY PAMPHLETS (DA PAM)
DA Pam 1-2, Personnel Administration Center (PAC) Guide
DA Pam 351-4, Army Formal Schools Catalog
DA Pam 351-20, Army Correspondence Course Program Catalog
DA Pam 600-11, Warrant Officer Professional Development
DA Pam 600-25, Noncommissioned Officer Professional Development Guide
DA Pam 601-110, Identification of Commissioned and Warrant Officer
        Personnel by Army Procurement Program Number Codes
DA Pam 611-279, Administration of Officer Selection Battery
DA Pam 611-282, Study Guide for OSB
DA Pam 621-200, Army Apprenticeship Procedural Guidance
DA Pam 623-205, The Noncommissioned Officer Evaluation Reporting
        System "in Brief"

FIELD MANUALS (FM)
FM 3-22.20, Physical Fitness Training
FM 6-22, Military Leadership
FM 3-22.9, Rifle Marksmanship, M16-/M4-Series Weapons
FM 1-04.1, Legal Guide for Commanders

MISCELLANEOUS SOURCES
American Council on Education. *The 2014 Guide to the Evaluation of Educational Experiences in the Armed Services*. Washington, D.C.: American Council on Education, 2014.
American Council on Education. *The National Guide to Educational Credit for Training Programs*. New York: MacMillan, 2014.
Dalessandro, Col. Robert J., US Army (Ret.). *The Army Officer's Guide*. 52nd Edition. Mechanicsburg, PA: Stackpole Books, 2013.
Educational Testing Service. *The College Board Guide to the CLEP Examinations*. New York: The College Board, 2015.
Jackson, Walter J., CSM, US Army (Ret.). *Soldier's Study Guide*. 7th Edition. Mechanicsburg, PA: Stackpole Books, 2013.
Rush, Robert S., CSM, US Army (Ret.). *Enlisted Soldier's Guide*. 7th Edition. Mechanicsburg, PA: Stackpole Books, 2006.
————. *NCO Guide*. 9th Edition. Mechanicsburg, PA: Stackpole Books, 2010.

TRAINING CIRCULAR
TC 3-22.20, Army Physical Readiness Training

Index

Page numbers in italics indicate figures, illustrations, etc.

STACKPOLE BOOKS

Military Professional Reference Library

as the availability of professor assistance. Fortunately, many college classes are available at lunchtime or after typical duty hours to meet even the most hectic schedules.

COLLEGE THROUGH CORRESPONDENCE
Like their military counterpart, college correspondence courses are an excellent resource for exportable education. It is possible to complete all of your degree requirements through correspondence courses. Numerous colleges offer extension programs or evaluation programs that accept this method of self-education.

Although some of these courses are completed in nearly the same manner as military courses, others require additional work. Typically, military courses are completed by passing an open-book examination provided at the back of the subcourse booklet. Many college correspondence courses require additional coursework, such as short term papers and writing projects. Some may even require closed-book examinations administered by a testing control officer on the installation.

Soldiers often prefer correspondence courses because they can be completed in any type of training environment. Even major deployments and similar field duty should not keep you from achieving your educational goals. Check with your local Education Center to find the most current programs available. Normally, tuition assistance is provided on a reimbursable basis for college correspondence course completion.

COLLEGE-LEVEL EQUIVALENCY EXAMINATIONS FOR CREDIT
Many college equivalency examinations, covering a wide range of topics and fields, are available to career-minded soldiers. These tests allow individuals to demonstrate that they have acquired the same level of knowledge that regular college students have in similar subjects. The tests can be used in a variety of ways. For instance, many soldiers use equivalency exams to verify personal experience or knowledge that is not documented elsewhere. Some soldiers find the tests useful as alternatives to the structured style of learning encountered in the classroom. These individuals often study subject matters on their own and then take the tests to validate their self-taught training.

Additionally, because the tests usually come from accredited institutions, many soldiers find equivalency exams very useful promotion tools. These official transcripts can be immediately placed in a soldier's personnel record and used for promotion credit. The tests count for the same credit as other college courses: 1 point for each semester hour earned. Common testing programs available to soldiers include the College-Level Examination Program (CLEP), Defense Activity for Non-Traditional Educational Support (DANTES), American College Testing Proficiency Examination Program (ACTPEP), Thomas Edison College Examination Program (TECEP), Regents College Examinations (RCE), and Graduate Record Examinations (GRE).

The following list gives some examples of individual exams that soldiers are often able to pass with no previous study. This list is definitely not complete and should be used only as a guide to stimulate further individual research.

Exam Title and Number	Source	Semester Hour Value
SP 562 Fundamentals of Counseling	DANTES	3
SE 532 Principles of Supervision	DANTES	3
SE 543 Introduction to Business	DANTES	3
SE 497 Introduction to Law Enforcement	DANTES	3
SD 539 Introduction to Management	DANTES	3
SE 756 Introduction to Carpentry	DANTES	3
SP 740 Basic Automotive Service	DANTES	3
SF 583 Beginning Spanish I	DANTES	3
SE 511 Environment and Humanity	DANTES	3
SD 457 History of West Civ to 1500	DANTES	3
SD 458 History of West Civ since 1500	DANTES	3
SE 424 Introductory College Algebra	DANTES	3
SE 821 Principles of Public Speaking	DANTES	3
SF 498 Criminal Justice	DANTES	3
SE 549 Basic Marketing	DANTES	3
SE 489 Foundations of Education	DANTES	3
SE 508 Here's to Your Health	DANTES	3
SF 531 Organizational Behavior	DANTES	3
SP 548 Money and Banking	DANTES	3
SE 935 Principles of Refrigeration	DANTES	3
American Literature	CLEP	3
Analysis & Interpretation of Literature	CLEP	3
English Literature	CLEP	3
Freshman English	CLEP	3
American Government	CLEP	3
American History to 1877	CLEP	3
American History 1865–Present	CLEP	3
Human Growth & Development	CLEP	3
Introductory Macroeconomics	CLEP	3
Introductory Microeconomics	CLEP	3
Introductory Sociology	CLEP	3
College Algebra	CLEP	3
General Biology	CLEP	3
General Chemistry	CLEP	3
Info Systems & Computer Applications	CLEP	3
Introduction to Management	CLEP	3
Introductory Accounting	CLEP	3

All of these tests have practice pretests available through the testing agencies and other related organizations. A score of 75 percent or better on the pretest would probably translate into a passing score on the actual test. General CLEP tests also are available in broader areas of study, such as humanities, social sciences and history, English, mathematics, and the natural sciences, and are worth 6 semester hours of credit each.

Choosing Equivalency Tests Wisely

Equivalency tests make good sense for many soldiers. Most education counselors encourage soldiers to start an individual study program by taking several of these tests. Usually the target tests are the general CLEP exams, because the Education Centers and post libraries often have a lot of study material to help soldiers prepare for these tests. Soldiers have been successfully taking these exams for a long time with good results. The only drawback is that most soldiers will have to invest several weeks of study time in order to pass most of the general CLEP exams. This is still faster than attending college, though, and has the advantage of being cost-free. In addition, you can study for these tests around any work schedule.

Be wise, however, about which exams you decide to challenge. Studying for one general CLEP exam may take you the same amount of time as it would to take and pass several individual exams. The best strategy is to go to your local Education Center and review all the tests available. Take pretests in every area that you think you might have some innate skill. Some of the results might surprise you. Then schedule and take each test for which you scored 75 percent or above on the pretest. If you do not pass the test but are close to achieving a passing score, spend a couple days reviewing the subject matter and then try again.

If you speak a foreign language, you can potentially earn up to 18 credit hours by passing the foreign language examinations. This is a wonderful way for soldiers whose second language is English to take advantage of their abilities in their native language.

WHAT TO EXPECT FROM AN ARMY EDUCATION COUNSELOR

Education counselors working in Army Education Centers or Army Learning Centers should be able to provide information and assistance on soldier career paths and methods of improving individual competencies. They can provide advice on college attendance, career choices, vocational programs, testing, foreign languages, tuition assistance, GI Bill benefits, and alternative funds for college. They should be able to help with all of your educational goals.

COLLEGE CREDIT FOR YOUR MILITARY EXPERIENCE

The American Council on Education (ACE) is a nationally recognized coordinating body for postsecondary education (education beyond high school). This council develops and influences credentialing guidelines, recommends educational credit, and operates several programs that assist agencies and institutions in providing recognition for skills, knowledge, and competencies gained through alternative means. Military members have benefited from the efforts of this coordinating body for more than fifty years. ACE is responsible for the evaluations of military training programs conducted through the service schools and similar training institutions. These evaluations have helped many soldiers receive college equivalent credit for their military training.

Evaluations are published in several ACE guides and are updated regularly. For soldiers, the most important of these guides is the *Guide to the Evaluation of Educational Experiences in the Armed Services*, which contains evaluations for military occupational specialty courses, basic training, NCOES courses, and many other formal courses offered by the Army, Army Reserve, and the Army National Guard. See the next page for a sample from this guide.

The Army/American Council on Education Registry Transcript System (AARTS)

AARTS is an automated system that is used for creating transcripts from military records of enlisted soldiers and some warrant officers. This database includes details of a soldier's military training and educational testing; this information is supplied to AARTS through several official sources. The unofficial transcripts on AARTS are designed to provide colleges and universities with an easy tool for determining credit awarded for military experience. The crediting recommendations are based on ACE guide evaluations, but the schools are not required to follow the recommendations. However, most postsecondary schools accept these recommendations and award civilian equivalent credit for these experiences.

Transcripts are available through the AARTS Operations Center. To request a transcript, fill out an application form (DD Form 295 or DA Form 5454-R) at your local Education Center. You also must submit a certified copy of your Personnel Qualifications Record (see your local Personnel Service Center). A sample AARTS transcript is available online at https://aarts.army.mil.

The same information can also be obtained through a Joint Services Transcript (JST) request. This service is available online at https://jst.doded.mil.

The eArmyU College Education Program

The Army recently launched an extensive online program called eArmyU, which makes postsecondary education available from virtually anywhere at any time. Under this umbrella, soldiers can obtain college degrees and have tuition costs covered in full. To qualify, Army enrollees must have at least three years' commitment remaining on their enlistment and agree to complete at least 12 semester hours of credit within a two-year period. (See the eArmyU Participation Agreement.) More information regarding this program is available at www.eArmyU.com.